One Foot in Front of the Other
A Widow's Journey

Cynthia P. Anderson LICSW

One Foot In Front Of The Other: A Widow's Journey was written after the untimely death of Cindy Anderson's husband, Ted. Her story carefully details the vigorous process of her personal search as it leads her to the ultimate spiritual mysteries of life. This book is not a gravesite monument to Ted, but rather a personal journey to a warm oasis of fond memories, new beginnings, and self-renewal.
Jay M. Morrison, MSW; LICSW
Boston College Graduate School of Social Work, Adjunct Faculty

One Foot In Front Of The Other: A Widow's Journey led me through the compelling experience of Cindy's widowhood with tears in my eyes and a smile on my face. I loved reading this book and found the mystical experiences very familiar. I joined the author on her journey through the joy of love, the shock of loss, the pain of grief, anger and loneliness, to resilience, endurance and finally, grace. Cindy's writing allows the reader to experience emotion in genuine and personal ways. This book is a primer on living your life well, loving fully and finding grace in self -reflection. In the end, it begs the question:
How do *you* wish to be remembered?
Mary "Smoki" Fraser
Human Resources Manager; Houghton Mifflin Co., Wilmington, MA

As a psychotherapist, former widow, and social work educator, I highly recommend Cynthia Anderson's new memoir *One Foot In Front Of The Other,* a moving story of oneness and compassion. This personal narrative includes photographs, references to relevant writings by others and spiritual encounters. Cynthia captures the depth of her compelling journey, writing with honesty and integrity. If you are involved with loss - professionally or personally - or are in the academic field, this book is well worth reading.
Jennifer Coplon, PhD, MSW
Adjunct Faculty, Salem State University, Graduate School of Social Work
Clinician, South End Community Health Center

Cynthia Anderson's sensitive recounting of a widow's journey will strike a responsive chord in all who have experienced loss. Her writing captures the innermost thoughts of a widow who gains strength and self-identity as she comes to believe in her own resilience. This is a thoughtful and joyful story.
Joanne Frolich, MSPED; Liaison: Wildflower Camp Foundation
Field Supervisor; Boston University, School of Education

This book is a testimony to the courage of the author who explores with unflinching honesty, pluck and sensitivity the raw grief when losing her beloved husband. Cindy fully shares her vulnerability and the wisdom she acquired that led her back from grief to living her life again with deeper joy and understanding. This poignant story will be an invaluable inspiration to those of us who can't imagine how we will survive one of life's most difficult transitions.
Brenda Prusak
Teacher/ Yoga Instructor

As a widow, I find *One Foot In Front Of The Other* to be a touching memoir; as a psychotherapist, I appreciate how Cindy reconstructs terrible grief into a new way of being.
Tanya White, Ph.D., A.B.P.P.

One Foot In Front Of The Other: A Widow's Journey should be in every library. This memoir takes the reader on the roller coaster journey into many facets of being a widow. Cindy is honest, candid and forthright, giving her full breadth of emotion while explaining her viewpoints with such clarity and feeling, I felt the reality of her experience. The concrete suggestions in "self help" are there for the taking. This should be a "must read" for any widow.
Joyce Collier Fearnside
Library Technician, Cary Memorial Library, Lexington, MA

One Foot In Front Of The Other is succinct, organized, profound and very real. Cindy is open about her feelings and shares her experiences in a fresh, uplifting way - both the highs and lows of loss. She gives many examples of her daily life and how she coped during her time of grieving.
Margie Quelet
Elementary School Teacher

As a recent widow, I found this book invaluable. The writer's authentic telling of her story resonates deeply with my own experiences. It was as if I'd discovered a comforting new friend in this writer. Cindy is someone I could sit down with over a cup of coffee and be reassured that my feelings and moods are quite normal. This validation is particularly important in a society that doesn't encourage the sharing of our grieving experiences openly the way other societies do. It really helped my own process of healing, and it will do so for many others. This book is a true gift from the heart to those of us who need it most.
Judy Cole
Educator

As a widow, I found Cindy's book a heartfelt narrative of surviving loss. *One Foot In Front Of The Other: A Widow's Journey* is a comforting companion during the time from grieving to healing.
Dianne Dahlbom, LICSW

I could not put this memoir down; it reads like a novel. Cindy offers an excellent guide for anyone in a state of bereavement, and anyone coping with and curious about death. When my mother died, I was considerably comforted with the supportive company of Joan Didion's book, *A Year of Magical Thinking*. Cindy's book, *One Foot In Front Of The Other* will bring the same peace to many widows. I appreciate the literary references throughout the text; it's clear that Cindy has done her research. I am struck by her honesty in trying to connect with her beloved. The author left no stone unturned in coming to terms with grief, allowing her to then move on and live her life. Whatever the reader's state of mind may be in, *A Widow's Journey* is a significant piece of shared humanity.
Judith Austin
Artist

I've been reading the inspiring and deeply - felt words in *One Foot In Front Of The Other* since early today. I couldn't put it down! How well Cindy writes of how she feels. Rarely have I felt so close to another's feelings. I am moved again and again. Although I'm not widowed yet, this book has refreshed what I still have while showing me that I can love even more in these days we have left, however many there are. Through conscious living, we feel, share, express and appreciate ever deeper and more lasting memories. In sharing her grief-struggle so well, Cindy has opened new doors of life and loving to me. Thank you, Cindy!
Jeanine Ellison Fisher, MSW, LCSW
School Social Worker, Psychotherapist, CMHC, Cherry Creek, Colorado

One Foot in Front of the Other
A Widow's Journey

Cynthia P. Anderson, LICSW

Honoring you
as you put
One foot in front of the other
Grace happens.
Warmly,
Cindy

ISBN # 1-5170440-0-6

Library of Congress Control Number: 2015912254
Summit Books, Lexington, MA

Cynthia P. Anderson, LICSW

One Foot in Front of the Other

A Widow's Journey

I. Psychology   II. Spiritual Memoir   III. Grief and Loss

IV. Paranormal

Printed in the United States of America

First printing February, 2015

Cover Photo:

Trail to Mohawk Lake near Breckenridge, Colorado

Dedication

I have always wondered what it was like for my grandmother when her beloved husband, my grandfather, died. My grandparents were soul mates, and I often think of my marriage to Ted as much like theirs. At the time my grandfather died I was only thirteen and oblivious to how my grandmother's heart must have been broken. Now, as I've gone through a similarly devastating loss and faced the future without my husband, I so often wonder what it was like for her.

And so I dedicate this book to my grandchildren – who one day may be curious to know, or may need to know because of some dark times in their own lives, what their "Grammy" went through. May it help them to know that, indeed, life does go on.

One Foot In Front Of The Other
A Widow's Journey

Part One: Gone

Part Two: Going On

"I am a husband and a widower,
An orphan and a father.
I am healthy and old.
Neither I nor we will last forever.
The Sun and Earth will too soon collapse.
Yet, I desperately hope to wake up with you now
...and again tomorrow."

Ted Anderson
April 18, 1996

Introduction

"Give sorrow words.
The grief that does not speak
whispers the o'erfraught heart and bids it break."

William Shakespeare
The Tragedy of Macbeth

When my husband died, I felt my life was over.

Oh, I knew my body would keep on working (although sometimes I doubted even that.) I'd eat. I'd sleep. I'd go to work, events would happen. The years would come and go and some day in the near or distant future I, too, would die. I moved through my days like a robot. Like the walking dead, I continued on physically, but the essence of what had given life its meaning, beauty, and zest was gone forever.

I could not imagine ever being truly happy again. My life with Ted, which had been so full of love and happiness, had ended abruptly. Ted was my sun, around which everything revolved. He was the hub of my life (my hubby!) When fate extracted the one key element, the essential ingredient, it seemed abundantly clear to me that true joy was no longer mine. It was a no-brainer. I felt like I'd never experience those peaks of happiness and intimacy again. From now on, I'd just be trying to make the best of a bad situation.

And yet something inside me resisted this fate. I had loved life. I loved loving. I loved the adventure. I loved the intimacy. I loved being happy. I didn't know how I was going to do it, but I simply *had* to create a meaningful life again. I was not willing to simply coast to the end.

And so, I read. I read fiercely, voraciously. I read countless books about death and grief and transformation. Books were my lifeline. I was especially drawn to books written by other widows (and widowers) who shared their stories about losing their spouses, and how they, too, had suffered, coped, and survived. Not only had they survived, but they went on to thrive. I felt desperate to know how this could be done. I wasn't so interested in reading about the stages of grief. I was familiar with all that. I wanted to know how I could create a miracle in my life. That's what I thought it would take to ever be happy again.

I found what I read extremely helpful. I didn't feel so alone in my grief. Waking up in the morning with a cup of hot coffee and a book (and then again at night settling into bed with my cup of hot tea and a book) was like drawing around the warmth of a campfire. The scary, cold darkness and loneliness were cast outside – at least temporarily. These stories of courage and strength warmed and comforted me. They helped me, and gave me the will to go on.

That's why I wrote this book. I have learned a lot along the way that I hope may be of help to others who are facing, or will face, this journey someday. Remarkable as it seems to me, I have gone on. The anguish I've gone through has transformed me. I have created a new life that I would not have dreamed possible. And for this, I feel grateful.

Part One:

GONE

"So many stars, all of them worlds,
Then at night one disappears.
Where has that ash or stone gone
Out there in a blackness of space?
How is it that light can dissolve?
In what form does it proceed?

Or, suddenly on a river or lake
A boat turns, a passenger sinks.
How is it that human life – good,
Generous, profoundly warm – how
Can something become nothing
Colder than water freezing?

How to move beyond vision
As we are gazing at a spot
Where a vessel left its track:
Our task is optimism, gladness,
Triumph through a kind action
Of simply loving and giving."

Kevin McGrath
(A rower friend of Ted's)
"For Ted Anderson" 2001

"There's Been An Incident On The River..."

"Life changes fast.
Life changes in the instant,
the ordinary instant.
You sit down to dinner
and life as you know it ends.

...Such an eerily casual way
that tragedy enters our everyday lives."
Joan Didion
The Year of Magical Thinking

July 14, 2001. Just a normal day. A day like any other summer day. Ted and I started off the morning in our usual manner with a cup of coffee in bed. I loved waking up with my husband this way – lying propped up on an assortment of pillows, sipping our coffee, holding hands and talking about our day ahead. Sometimes we watched the morning news on TV, but more often we enjoyed the quiet and just being together before we went our separate ways for the day. On this particular day, I was going to be doing a signing for a book I'd recently published, *Pioneer Voices, from Plymouth to Breckenridge*, which is the story of my family, the Peabody's, as they

migrated over the course of eleven generations from New England To Colorado. Ted faced challenges of his own that morning as he was heading off to row in a sculling race on the Merrimac River. I was aware that he seemed a little tense and I wished I were free to go with him. I ordinarily went to his races to cheer him on, but because of the book signing, I wasn't able to be with him this day.

Ted had retired a year earlier from his private practice in clinical psychiatry and from consulting at the Massachusetts General hospital. Since then, he had taken up rowing with a passion. I had still been working as a clinical social worker. Ted had decided to use his newly-found freedom to pursue this sport he'd enjoyed in his college days at Harvard fifty years earlier. He worked out vigorously all winter, rowed daily in the summer, and entered as many races as possible. His goal was to do well in both the World Rowing Championships in Montreal later that summer, and the Head of the Charles race that fall. That previous weekend, he had been disappointed by his performance in a 1,000-meter race on the Charles River, so he had signed up for this additional race on the Merrimack hoping to improve his time.

That morning in 2001, Ted dressed in his Cambridge Boat Club shirt and his sleek rowing shorts. Even after 33 years of marriage, I enjoyed watching him dress. I admired his beautifully muscled body and thought he looked very sexy as he pulled on his skin-tight racing shorts. When Ted walked out the door that morning my farewell was, "I love you." Not, "Good luck, have a good time," as I often said.

"I love you" were not the words we chose for our usual goodbye to each other when one of us left for the day. We saved this farewell for when one of us was going away on a long trip, but not when we were going to be gone for three or four hours. In fact, I had never before said, "I love you," to Ted when he went off to row in a race – even a big one, which this race was not.

After Ted left, I went off to do some grocery shopping before going down to the bookstore. I had just returned home and was walking in the door carrying two big bags of fruit and vegetables from the local farm stand when I heard the phone ringing.

"There's been an incident on the river," the innocuous-sounding voice began. "Your husband has had a heart attack."

My heart lurched in my throat as my mind moved quickly to fill in the blanks, skipping ahead in my planning. *Yes, we can deal with this,* I thought. He'd been in the hospital before: two operations on his knee, a scary blood disease many years ago, and a hernia operation. We'd been down this road before, in the hospital for a few days, and then a period of recuperation at home. *We can do this.* The voice interrupted my thoughts.

"Maybe you should get in your car and come on up to the hospital. On second thought, just wait until we call you again."

Hanging up, I sat in a daze. What was I supposed to do? Then it occurred to me to call our daughter, Sandy, and our son, Brett.

As I spoke to them, my words sounded unreal. I said I'd call them back as soon as I knew more. I waited another minute or two. I was feeling confused and disorganized. My brain was buried in a thick fog. Deep in my chest, ominous rumblings of fear began. Panic was setting in. I finally gathered my forces and thought, *I'll call the hospital myself.*

The voice on the other end confirmed.

"Yes, we have Ted Anderson here."

The voice began asking a lot of inane questions like what was his date of birth; what medications he was taking; did he have a heart condition? Finally I interrupted him to ask, "So how <u>is</u> he?!"

And at that moment I noticed a police car had driven into my driveway. I mentioned this to the person on the phone and she asked to speak to the policeman, whom I had by now let into the house. I handed the phone to the officer. My heart began to pound. After a moment of conferring, he hung up and delivered the words that shattered my world and irrevocably changed the course of my life.

"Your husband didn't make it, Mrs. Anderson. He died."

My reaction was not to burst into tears. A flash of anger sliced through my head: *You rowed yourself to death!*

For a fraction of a moment, I felt an irrational sense of vindication. *See, I was right to have worried so much about how you pushed yourself!*

This thought was as quickly followed by self-recrimination. *What a terrible thing to think!*

Then shock set in. This news was incomprehensible. The only words that found their way out were, "Oh, my goodness, oh, my goodness!"

At about that time, Sandy drove up. She ran across the driveway and into the house. I had to look into her panic-stricken eyes and tell her that her dad had died. She immediately burst into tears and became hysterical. A few of my own tears found their own escape, but for the most part, I was in a daze. Numb. The policeman kindly drove us to Lowell General Hospital. We never could have made it there on our own. But first, I had the horrible task of having to call Brett and deliver the news that his father didn't make it. Brett said he'd meet us at the hospital.

As we drove together, the policeman told us he had known Ted personally. He spoke fondly of how Ted had once given him an old broken lawn mower to repair in his side business of repairing snow blowers and lawn mowers. They shared a love of repairing small engines.

I hardly remember the drive to the hospital. Sandy and I sat in the back seat mostly in stunned silence. I was in a thick fog. Everything felt surreal. *This just can't be true. I must be having a bad dream. Surely I'll wake up any moment now. PLEASE.*

This Must Be A Bad Dream

"Midnight. No waves
no wind. The empty boat
is flooded with moonlight. "

Dogen
Zen and the Art of Anything

When Sandy and I arrived at the hospital in the police car, our son, Brett, and his wife, Barbara, were waiting there. A doctor tried to explain to us what had happened and what they'd done. I couldn't hear a word he said; layers and layers of thick fog enveloped me. Then someone ushered me in to see Ted one last time. I could not believe this was happening, like a scene out of some horror movie. There he was, my poor husband, his body lying on a stretcher with a tube down his throat. Apparently, the tube had to remain there until they did the autopsy. Already his body was cold except under his armpits where I could feel a little warmth remaining. His hands and fingers were still soft and pliable. I held his big, big hands in mine, but this time they didn't squeeze me back. I laid my head on his chest and hugged him and just wept. I couldn't even kiss his lips because of that stupid tube. I held him and hugged him and touched him and remembered all the joy his wonderful body had given me. Oh, the fun we'd had together! I just couldn't believe it... my husband... dead? How could this be? I was stunned.

As I think about it now, I wish I had stayed with him longer. I don't know why I felt the pressure to hasten this final goodbye. Perhaps Sandy and Brett would have liked some time alone with their dad too. Why did I feel the need to accommodate the hospital or the policeman waiting outside the door?

Then, we were faced with having to go to the boathouse on the Merrimack River to retrieve his belongings. Ted's car, racing shell and personal effects were not going to be magically transported home. Having to go there forced us to see where on the river "the incident" had occurred. The river was surprisingly wide where he had crossed the finish line and gone down – maybe even a quarter of a mile across. Ted had been rowing in the far lane on the far, far side of the river, which is to say my husband was way out of reach...and all alone out there on the water.

As I talked to various people, I began to piece together the story of what had happened. Ted had arrived at the rowing regatta that morning and discovered, to his surprise and consternation, that his event was a 2,000-meter race, not a 1,000. He had remarked to a couple of other rowers before race time, "How do you row a 2,000? I've never done this before!"

In the Head of the Charles, a three-mile-long race that he'd rowed several times, the rowers pace themselves for the long haul. A 1,000-meter race is a short race, and rowers sprint as fast as they can to the finish line. Ted must have found himself at the starting line having just realized he had to row twice as far as he'd expected. He had no time to plan how to row his hardest and yet pace himself for a mid-length race. He probably sprinted the entire way, exactly as he had done the previous weekend. Ironically, he did cross the finish line first in his heat, but then he collapsed.

I later talked to a friend of Ted's who had rowed in the same heat. He said, after crossing the finish line, he had glanced across the river and seen Ted's boat upside down with Ted nowhere in sight. He instantly worried that Ted was underneath his racing shell with his feet still clamped to his boat. This friend had managed to turn his own boat around (which took some doing because racing shells are long and unwieldy) and had rowed across the river to where Ted's boat had capsized. He had jumped into the water, but because the river was so deep, he had found nothing solid to stand on.

His worst fears were confirmed when he found Ted still attached to his shell and immobile. This friend had a lot of difficulty pulling Ted's body up from underneath his boat while trying to keep his own head above water. He had struggled while waiting for the rescue boat to arrive. The security motorboat had followed Ted's heat down the river, but as soon as the rowers had crossed the finish line, the emergency boat had turned around to go back to follow the next heat. No one had noticed what had happened to Ted. I was told that by the time the rescue boat finally did come back to help Ted, at least 15 minutes had elapsed. An eternity. If I'd been standing on the shore watching that nightmare unfold, I would have died a thousand deaths. Somehow, fate had spared me being more traumatized than I already was.

Ultimately, the rescue boat did arrive and more precious minutes were lost by the inept attempts of the race officials to get his body into the boat. The two strongest men had jumped into the deep water leaving the smallest, weakest man in the motorboat. With nothing on which to gain their footing, the men in this deep water had a hard time lifting Ted up to the man in the rescue boat who wasn't strong enough to pull him up. By the time they finally got Ted to the ambulance, many more

precious minutes had been wasted. The doctor I spoke to at the hospital told me that Ted still had a slight pulse as the paramedics worked on him in the ambulance, but they couldn't revive him.

As I heard more of the details of this catastrophe within the catastrophe, I was furious with the race officials. Why had they been so incompetent in responding to the crisis? Why didn't they have a defibrillator in the rescue boat? But, in retrospect, it probably didn't matter. If his heart had gone into ventricular fibrillation, which is what a rower friend who is also a physician thought had happened, Ted would have needed a defibrillator within 3 or 4 minutes. Slow or fast, nothing could have saved him.

Sandy, Brett and I did what we had to do and made our way home; for the first time home to the empty house. One of the saddest things I've ever had to do was to then call my other two children and tell them the awful news that their father had died. Ironically, Karyn and Scott had both been involved in athletic adventures of their own that day, challenging their bodies and celebrating the joy of being alive. Karyn had been kayaking with several of her friends on a lake in Maryland. Scott had been competing in the Triple By-Pass Bicycle event; a grueling 135-mile ride over three 14,000'- high, mountain passes in the Colorado Rockies. He had just peddled into a rest station after completing the second of the three passes when his wife, children, and our good friends intercepted him and told him the terrible news.

The rest of that awful day somehow unfolded. Instinctively, I reached out to two or three of my good friends.

"I need your help. Something awful has happened. Ted has died!"

I couldn't believe the words I heard coming out of my mouth. I also called my minister, Helen Cohen, who dropped everything and arrived at my door just a half-hour later, wet hair and all. We set the necessary details in motion.

And so the day passed – the worst day of my life. But not before delivering its final blow, my having to crawl into our big, king-size bed alone. I reached out my arm to Ted's side of the bed, but no one was there. Just a few short hours before, we had so happily snuggled here, contentedly taking for granted our being together, and now it was all over. I would never hold him again. The tears finally came.

Saying Goodbye

"The awe and innocence of simply not knowing."

Ted Anderson

The following few days passed in a blur. Events had their own momentum, starting with a deluge of arrivals. My two out-of-state children, Karyn and Scott, and their families flew in the next day. Colleagues and friends stopped by to extend their kindness. Flowers appeared; cards and letters filled my mailbox. A steady stream of casseroles and desserts kept arriving, as well as countless platters of broccoli, celery and carrot sticks (most of which I put straight into a bag in the freezer to be reincarnated months later in a big pot of vegetable soup). I lost track of all that came into the house. Many people went un-thanked for their generosity; some dishes never found their way back to their rightful owner. I have to hope they understood that I was not in my right mind.

I was so appreciative of my friends who dropped everything in their own lives and took over what had to be done: notifying our friends of Ted's death, arranging for the reception after the memorial service and calling my patients and cancelling my appointments. Most important, they were there with me. So many loving people surrounded me. Except the one who mattered most.

We held the memorial service four days after Ted's death. What a strange experience to walk into the Unitarian Universalist Church that day. I remembered visiting this pretty white church on the green in Lexington, Massachusetts, 37 years ago, long before I had met Ted. I was still a graduate student at the University of Denver at that time, but had come out to Cohasset, Mass., to work for the summer. Little did I dream that one day I'd be living in this town and attending this church; little did I know that I'd be attending the burial service for my future husband in this very same church.

I felt like the walking dead as I made my way into the church. Numbly, I followed the rest of the family – my children, their spouses, my grandchildren, my two nieces, nephew and cousin – into the sanctuary as we took our seats in the first two rows. I kept thinking, *it's time for this nightmare to be over*. I glanced around and noticed the room was packed. People filled the balcony and were standing up against the back wall. I wondered how they all knew that Ted had died. Staring at us on a little table in the front of the congregation was a marble urn. How bizarre to know my husband was in that jar – my husband, now turned to ash. Behind it had been placed a larger-than-life sized photo of Ted in his rowing jersey, showing his beautifully muscled arms and shoulders and his big, dazzling smile. He simply radiated his love of life.

I was so proud of my children and amazed that they had the courage, in the midst of their anguish, to stand up and speak. They hadn't decided until just beforehand to address all the people who had come to pay their respects.

Brett, our youngest, said he'd written out a few words. His intention to publicly honor his father may have been the catalyst that pushed the others to do likewise. Karyn suggested that they go in birth order. As Sandy said in her opening words to the audience, "This is the first time in all my life I wish I was the twin who was born seven minutes after my brother, Scott. I regret having boasted so many times about being born first."

Sandy continued, telling about the amazing experience she had at the end of that horrible day in which she learned her father had died. She said to all of us gathered there that morning:

"I saw an incredible, bold, beautiful, straight-down rainbow on my way home from my house that fateful day." As she got closer to her home, she saw another beautiful rainbow, however this time it had been a double rainbow. She told all of us at the service that she had said to herself, "If I can still see a rainbow when I get home, I'll believe it was Dad. But when I got home, I was so anxious to see my family that I forgot to look. I am left with the *'awe and the innocence of simply not knowing'* that my father had spoken about."

Then Scott spoke admiringly of the passion with which his dad had lived his life, and how at the very moment Ted was rowing his heart out (literally), ironically he, Scott, had been competing in his own grueling bicycle race.

"We had both been giving one hundred percent. And that's kind of comforting to me – that's the kind of dad I had," Scott said.

Karyn went on to talk about another of Ted's passions – banjo playing. They had developed a special closeness around his teaching her to play. There was sadness and a little bitterness in her words to us:

Sadly and a little bitterly she said, "At this very time, he was supposed to be picking me up at the airport to go to a Blue Grass Festival in upstate New York. This is not the way it's supposed to be."

And lastly, Brett spoke in simple but poignant words about the ingredients he had learned from his father about how to lead a good life.

"Dad taught me to think mechanically; how completely clearing a dinner plate gives a complement to the chef –my mother; how helping a stranger on the side of the road can make one's day. Dad taught me how to be a strong, yet tender man."

They spoke from their heart, each expressing a different facet of Ted's spirit.

I knew that there was no way I could ever get up and speak. If I were to attempt it, I imagined I would either just start sobbing or I'd be so numb that I would say a few robotic-like sentences and would fail miserably to do justice to the husband I wanted to honor. My minister had given me a wonderful idea. I could write something, a letter to Ted, which she would read for me. I was grateful for the idea.

I wrote about the disbelief I felt, how I wandered around the house thinking Ted would walk in the door at just any moment. I saw him as a part of everything – the piles of papers strewn on the study floor, the VW camper parked in the driveway, his raggedy blue jean cut-offs still lying on the bedroom chair, the granddaddy tree in the backyard, the banjo, the tools, the mountains, the sky, the everywhere – and yet he was nowhere. I couldn't wrap my mind around it.

I told about the anger I felt for his letting rowing matter so much. But that suddenly in the middle of the night, I had said to myself, "I realize you were simply doing what you do. You were living life with passion, to the fullest. There is no way you could have known that this day would turn out differently than any other day when you were simply trying to do your best."

I also acknowledged how deeply grateful I was for our 35 years together.

"But I am greedy; I was looking forward to years and years more; I wanted to grow really old with you...be two crotchety old folks, sitting in our rocking chairs on the front porch."

"The heavens wept the day you died, but I am also strangely comforted by the rainbow that had appeared over the field. Rev. Cohen tells me that a rainbow is a sign of promise. Your life overarched many worlds. You spread your radiant spirit to many corners of the earth. There is so much we don't know about life and death. I guess rather than finding answers, it just remains a mystery. Or in your words, *'The awe and innocence of simply not knowing.'"*

"You are the light and love of my life. You will be with me forever."

Ted's Parting Gift

"Rainbow – a messenger from another realm"

Eckhart Tolle
A New Earth

Ted did not believe in the hereafter. He often said, "When you die, you're dead. That's it. End of story." In fact, he thought that staking one's hopes for happiness on a life to come after death keeps people from fully living <u>this</u> life. I wasn't so sure.

We'd had many a "discussion" on this subject. I read that Elisabeth Kübler-Ross and her doctor-husband had similar differences of opinion over the possibility of consciousness continuing after the physical death of the body. Elisabeth asked him, *"If you die before me and there is something more, send me a sign."*

Then one day, he suffered a cardiac arrest and died suddenly. Elizabeth arrived home and found a beautiful red rose lying on her doorstep in the snow. This was apparently of significance between them; she took it as her husband's way of communicating the existence of something beyond death.

I once asked a similar request of my husband: if there *is* something beyond this life, send me some kind of sign. Ted sent me rainbows. Sandy's speaking at the memorial service of seeing the rainbows on the day her father died sparked a number of people to come forward with their sightings of rainbows on the day of his death. Two rowers attending the service who had been racing with Ted on the Merrimack River told us that, as they were standing on the dock at the end of the race day, they saw a *"magnificent double rainbow appear over the river. The first rainbow arched high in the sky and the second arc skimmed the water, just where Ted had gone down earlier that day."* As the last rowers finished their races and paddled back to the boathouse, they passed through this double rainbow. Later, I received a card from the race officials who confirmed having seen the same phenomenon – a double rainbow over the river where Ted had gone down. I was utterly astonished. Could it be just coincidence, or was something more going on? Such an unexpected gift in the midst of our raw sorrow.

Karyn had her own rainbow story to tell. A day or two after Ted's death, she had a "14 Rainbow Dream." In her dream she was driving by a field with me. She saw over the field many, many rainbows. She counted 1, 2, 3, 4, 5...13, 14 rainbows! In her dream, she said, "Look Mom!" And together we counted them again. Fourteen rainbows!

Later, we wondered what did 14 signify? Suddenly it occurred to us that Ted had died on July 14.

A cascade of other rainbow stories soon followed. Three days before Ted's death, the *Boston Globe* had published the photo of a gorgeous rainbow over

Dorchester Bay on the front page. On the day of his death, some friends were so moved by the beauty of a rainbow they saw in New Hampshire, that they stopped to take a photograph and later made a copy for me. On the same day, another friend saw a spectacular rainbow while driving on the Maine turnpike. When he told his wife about it, she also reported having seen a gorgeous rainbow that afternoon over Lake Sebago. Later in the day, when these friends learned that Ted had died that morning, they were struck by the strange coincidence of his passing and their seeing the rainbows.

On the day of Ted's memorial service, another friend told of having seen a magnificent rainbow while driving home from the service. What he thought especially startling about the presence of this rainbow was that the sun was brightly shining and there had not been any rain that day. Then two days after the service at a family gathering at my daughter Sandy's house in Lincoln, my cousin and I walked down the trail to the lake.

As we stood on the dock I said to Jeanie, "Wouldn't it be nice to see a rainbow right now?" And then as we gazed out at the lake we noticed a spectrum of colors lying on the water, and looking up into the sky we saw the small wedge of a rainbow nestled in the clouds!

A month or so after Ted's death, I had another treat. As I sat in my car waiting to go in to my first bereavement group, I saw the arc of an absolutely huge, dazzling rainbow stretching across the sky from one horizon to the other. My aching heart filled with joy.

I knew Ted had sent it, and imagined what he would say to me if he could:

"Do I have to send you anymore? What does it take for you to believe that my spirit is still here with you? There is more going on than you can see."

Now, you can say the viewing of these rainbows were all just coincidental, and maybe so. In Colorado and the Southwest, one frequently sees a rainbow after an afternoon thunderstorm, but not here in the Boston area. The sheer abundance and concentration in time of this many rainbows around Ted's death was nothing short of astonishing. This fits the definition of *synchronicity*, a word that Swiss psychologist Carl Jung defined as "a meaningful coincidence of two or more events, where something other than the probability of chance is involved." In his book, *The Portable Jung*, Joseph Campbell wrote of how Jung distinguished this from mere causality, the standard way of explaining the link between two successive events. He wrote:

"Synchronicity designates the parallelism of time and meaning between psychic and psychophysical events... The term explains nothing, it simply formulates the occurrence of meaningful coincidences which, in

themselves, are chance happenings, but are so improbable that we must assume them to be based on some kind of principle, or on some property of the empirical world."

What Jung is saying is that these synchronicities are not mystical or inexplicable events, but are simply based on empirical principles that we haven't yet fully understood or codified.

In the following years, rainbows often appeared at significant moments when I traveled. In Thailand, after coming across a rowing regatta on a river, a rainbow appeared. While gingerly crossing a high canopy walkway in the Amazon jungle, a rainbow peeked through the palm trees. And on the Sahara desert, after climbing to the top of the starkly beautiful sand dunes, I was overjoyed to see a rainbow on the distant horizon.

I like to think of the synchronicity of the rainbows as part of the mystery; a promise sent to me from Ted that says *more exists than we can see*. The rainbow serves as a bridge for me to the realm beyond – where Ted's spirit lives on. (I'll have more to say on the subject of synchronicity in Part 3 of this book.)

> *"In Tibetan Buddhism, the fact that the rainbow exists – a vivid array of many colors, yet insubstantial, born of light – has made it a symbol of the true nature of life. To see one is considered auspicious, an indication of blessings from the Buddha, bodhisattvas, teachers or deities."*

Sharon Salzberg
Faith

Scattering The "Remains"

Ted and I never talked much about what to do after our deaths. We had never looked into buying a cemetery plot. All I knew was that he wanted to be cremated. But as far as anything else – the service, where to scatter his ashes – Ted just said that the wishes of the living should be honored, not the concerns of the person who's dead. So I had no idea what to do with him. A few days after he died, the mortuary had called and said I needed to choose the container I wanted for my husband's remains. To think my vibrant, robust, and so-very-alive husband had now been reduced to a container of "remains!" What had become of his essence, his very aliveness? Was he simply gone, evaporated? *But I've got a job to do*, I said to myself. *I can't be wondering about these things now.*

I had never realized how many choices I had. Did I want a lovely blue ceramic keepsake urn beautifully painted with wildflowers? Or should I choose a handsome mahogany or rosemary box carved with mountains or dolphins; or perhaps a handsome bronze, pewter or marble urn? The mortician said it could be pleasingly decorated with praying hands, a cross or hummingbirds (or, I thought, *how about a raised, clenched fist!)* Or perhaps I'd like a biodegradable urn for a burial at sea? How the hell did I know! The fact was I didn't want any of them. I wanted my husband back, alive and in the flesh.

In the end, the mortician played upon my guilt sufficiently enough that I chose a gray marble urn with his name and birth and death dates etched on it. The mortician clucked approvingly, "An impressive urn appropriate for a man of his stature." After all, I didn't want to appear chintzy at the memorial service where it would be displayed. Ted would have preferred for Scott and Brett to nail together a little box made out of plywood in the basement. Later. I had told my children that someday they could use the same urn for me and save themselves the money and aggravation.

My friend Jennifer had offered to come with me to pick up the urn and I am glad I took her up on it. I had been feeling detached and unemotional as I went into the mortuary and carried the big, heavy marble urn with the ashes of my husband out to the car. Then, suddenly it hit me. "This is my husband! My poor husband! This is all so wrong – taking you home like this." I cried and cried. Later, I went out to dinner with friends. When I came home, that stupid urn was sitting on the counter staring at me. "I don't want a cold, hard, sterile, lifeless piece of stone filled with ashes! I want *you*! Where the hell *are* you?!"

After much thought and discussion, my children and I had decided that we would scatter his ashes up on Mt. Washington. Ever since Ted had been a young man in college, he had loved hiking its many trails and skiing the famous "head wall." He had often said that he wanted to celebrate his 80th birthday by hiking up to the summit of Mt. Washington with any of our friends and family who could join him. It seemed the natural thing to do to was to take his ashes up there. Sadly, he would only able to be with us in spirit.

Granddaddy Tree

I also wanted to feel that I had some of his ashes closer to me. So before the Mt. Washington ceremony, I decided to scatter some of his ashes around the big Granddaddy Tree in the backyard. This giant black maple that had dominated our

back yard was dear to Ted's heart. I had asked Helen Cohen, the minister of the Unitarian church, to join me, and the two of us created a little ceremony. I brought out a couple of chairs and a little table, made a pot of tea for us, and placed the urn with its "remains" at the base of the tree. I hadn't prepared much in the way of a ceremony, just a couple of poems and a letter I'd written to Ted, and Helen brought a reading. But mostly we just sat. We sat and allowed the spirit of the moment to unfold.

I told Helen how Ted had sometimes enjoyed sitting on the back deck and meditating with "his" tree. He'd had fun imagining that he and the tree were breathing in "unison" – as he breathed in oxygen from the tree and exhaled carbon dioxide, the tree took in his carbon dioxide and breathed out oxygen. They lived with each other in harmony and mutual dependence. We were struck by how this Granddaddy of all trees now resembled Ted's spirit. Its deep roots reminded me of his depth. Ted didn't just live on the *surface* of life. Ted was a deep thinker, a teacher and an avid learner, forever curious about the workings of the world.

I also thought about how the tree's enormous trunk reminded me of Ted's strength and solidity. When I had self-doubts or came home after a bad day, Ted had been my haven in the storm. I could always count on him to be understanding with me. He had always seen the good in people, all people.

Helen listened as I shared the memory of a terrible time in the past, when a colleague's daughter and grandchildren had been brutally murdered by her husband. Ted had gone to the trial to be a support to his friend. However, he had also felt great compassion for the man who had committed this heinous crime. Ted had reached out to him and tried to enlist others to do likewise. I don't think he had gotten many to join him.

I wondered now with the loss of my husband – whose presence had given us such strength – would we all collapse? Or were his roots still here, hidden beneath the surface? Would we someday rediscover his spirit that may still be underneath and within us all?

Helen and I talked about such things. I told her about how much fun Ted had building a long swing for his grandchildren and hanging it from his tree's sturdy branches. To me, the swing represented Ted's playful spirit and how much he had loved his grandchildren. Sometimes he'd set up a ladder so the children could climb up into its lower limbs. Another time, he'd had fun with them by squirting water into some of the Granddaddy Tree's higher holes and flushing the "crud" out of its lower holes. They had all laughed and talked about how this had made the old tree feel so much better.

As I shared these memories of my life with Ted, we shed many tears. We even had a few good laughs as we imagined Ted watching us and giving us his "helpful advice" as we struggled to set up the big, old, awkward ladder and lean it against the tree so that I could climb up into the lower branches and pour some ashes down its ancient holes – much like he had done with his grandchildren and the water. Like the tree, I felt so much better after our little ceremony.

Mt. Washington

All four of our children came home Columbus Day weekend to participate in the Mt. Washington ceremony. We decided to camp at the base of the mountain and then hike up the trail until we found a good spot to scatter the ashes. As we packed up, we felt like we were preparing for a "good-old-days" Anderson camping trip – gathering sleeping bags and tents, shopping for food, getting out the old camp stove and all our hiking gear.

Finally, we were all loaded up and ready to go. As we locked up the house and walked out to the camper, someone exclaimed, "We forgot Dad!" In our excitement, we had forgotten to pack the urn.

Scott carried the precious burden up the hill. The marble urn was heavy, and I was surprised at how heavy the ashes themselves were. I had suggested to Scott that we might re-pack the ashes to make his load lighter. But he insisted on carrying the whole thing as it was. This had to be a sad but tender experience for Scott – carrying his father on his back up the mountain, reminiscent of when he was a little boy and his dad had carried him on his back on many a hiking trip.

We hiked from our campground at the bottom of Mt. Washington all the way up until we found a beautiful spot, high above timberline, in an area called the Alpine Garden. It had been a long time since I had climbed from the bottom, and I was pleased that I was able to make it up the challenging Lion's Head Trail. Looking out at a gorgeous view of the distant mountains, we held our little ceremony. We played music, read poetry, and I read a goodbye letter I'd written to Ted. I also wrote a letter to each of my children telling them how I see them, each in their own way, embodying Ted's spirit.

We had just finished scattering his ashes when Sandy exclaimed, "Look, there's a bear up on those rocks!" As we looked more closely we saw a pair of bears high up on the mountain, just below the summit, ambling along on the rocky hillside. To see a couple of bears roaming around on exposed rocks high above tree line is an extremely rare occurrence. You might expect to see a mountain goat or sheep or marmot, but not a bear. In all my years of hiking, I have never actually seen a bear out in the wild. Since then, I've asked a number of mountaineers how common it would be for bears to be in this kind of terrain, high above timberline, roaming about on open, exposed rock. They all agreed that it is highly unlikely. Synchronicity? Was it some kind of message, like the rainbow? A bear would have been a good symbol for Ted. The bear is a profound Native American symbol of majesty, power and freedom of spirit, as is the great wind. I particularly like the Native Crow Indian symbolism of the bear:

"I may jump among high cliffs and I shall never die."

Should I Have Seen It Coming?

"When his boat snapped loose
from its mooring, under
the screaking of the gulls,
he tried at first to wave
to his dear ones on shore,
but in the rolling fog
they had already lost their faces.
Too tired even to choose
between jumping and calling,
somehow he felt absolved and free
of his burdens, those mottoes
stamped on his name-tag:
conscience, ambition, and all
that caring.
He was content to lie down
with the family ghosts
in the slop of his cradle,
buffeted by the storm,
endlessly drifting.
Peace! Peace!
To be rocked by the Infinite!
as if it didn't matter
which way was home;
as if he didn't know
he loved the earth so much
he wanted to stay forever."

Stanley Kunitz
"The Long Boat"

I was not armed with any worry as Ted went off to row on that particular morning. It was like a hundred other mornings. We knew of no medical reason why we should be concerned about his pushing his body and rowing as vigorously as his spirit would allow. Although he had faced a few chronic health concerns – a problematic right knee, well-controlled high blood pressure and low-grade hepatitis – none of these had been immanent or life-threatening. Ted had always prided himself on having a big, strong athletic heart with its unusually slow heartbeat. He was accustomed to exercising strenuously with men ten to twenty years younger. In the winter, he had been accustomed to working out on the rowing machine, and had run up and down the stadium steps with his friends. In the summer, he had been up early every morning and out rowing on the Charles River, perfecting his stroke and building his endurance. His buddies at the Cambridge Boat House admiringly referred to his beautifully muscled arms and legs as his "pipes." One handsome hunk of a man, my husband was.

The night before his death, we had celebrated our 33rd wedding anniversary by attending the Boston Pops with the Massachusetts Medical Society. It was just an okay night – filing past long buffet tables laden with kettles of non-descript-looking food, then standing around and balancing plates and plastic wine glasses while we tried to make conversation over the blare of annoying background music with people we didn't know very well and didn't care to know well. Later, as we sat with other couples around a little table listening to the concert, I thought, *This is certainly not the most romantic anniversary we've ever had...but there's always next year.* We've all endured such evenings, but to make such a choice on my anniversary night had felt like a mistake.

As we had gone to bed that night, Ted had asked me to use the vibrator to massage his neck and shoulders, an unusual request. Should I have sensed something ominous in the making? Ted was a pretty laid-back guy and I don't remember his ever having asked me for help in order to relax before. In retrospect, he *had* seemed a little tense and preoccupied that night. Why had this race been so damned important, anyway?

I went to sleep that night happy, deliciously snuggled in our spoon position, blissfully unaware that I was spending the last night of my life with my sweetheart. But I suppose life has a way of protecting us. If we knew some disaster was one day going to ambush us, we'd spend our days anticipating the tragedy that was lying in wait within every shadow and behind every bush.

Had it also been a forewarning when, a week or so earlier, Ted had awoken one morning and shared a disconcerting dream that he'd had? He rarely had frightening dreams, but this one was a nightmare. He had spoken of terrible scenes of ambulances and sirens and fire engines coming. Had these been the early rumblings of disaster in the making? The images had been so disturbing that we hadn't delved into the dream at all to explore its possible interpretations. As a psychiatrist and a clinical social worker, it was in our natures to be fascinated by the workings of the unconscious. Understanding the meaning of dreams was what we did. But not that dream! We hadn't wanted to touch it.

"Forget it – it was just a dream," we had both said. Looking back now, I wonder if that dream was bringing us a message of what was lurking down the road.

And then there was the last piece Ted had written, just six days before he died:

"What are you doing?
I'm writing a book.
On what?

Thoughts that interest me. I've had some interesting thoughts stimulated by my interactions with my patients, family and friends. And often when I tell them to others, they find them useful. And I like that. It makes me feel less lonely.

Like what thoughts?

Oh, like when a good friend dies, people are sad and a bit disoriented. So am I. I've had some serious losses in my life, and when this happened I noticed that I had not lost anything that I'd had with that person. What we had done together would always have been. I didn't lose that at all. So what was lost? I certainly felt like I'd lost something.

What I had lost was the future in which that person was a part. In fact, every future I had anticipated had that person in it. Now all those possible futures had disappeared and I had to create the array of possible futures in which that person didn't exist. It was the future with that person that was lost."

Ted Anderson
July 8, 2001

I had also come across another of Ted's writings, a longer exposition titled *"Thoughts on my mortality,"* dated July 1, 2001. In this piece of writing written just two weeks before his death, Ted seemed to be working hard to understand what would become of him when he died. An excerpt:

"...When I die my mind and body come apart. No matter what form of immortality I conceive, it can't possibly be the same as the "me" I'm aware of existing in real time-space. Either I continue in the memories of others (and we know how distorted that is,) or blend with the universal consciousness (losing the distinctness of me vs. not-me) or reincarnate (again, losing the "me" identity that I know so well) or go to heaven or hell (where I lose the same body sensation, and where the rules of time-space are presumably all different.) No matter how I twist and turn my theories of after-life, they don't preserve the "me" uniqueness which I am familiar with and which I have come to love and which I have tried to preserve.

No, I must confess, preserving the "me" that I know and love, and which exists and which I have defined in relationship with the "not-me" is simply impossible. I must say goodbye forever. And also to the world and universe that I have always known in relationship to me. They may or may not go on after I die (I'll never know). But for sure they will be

25

without me. And that means the universe that goes on will be unlike the one that I know and love so well. I must say goodbye to it all... The effect of one man leaving is dramatically experienced. When we leave, the world becomes unrecognizable in ways that we could not have predicted. It is truly a different world..."

Were these two pieces of Ted's writings yet another example of synchronicity? He seems to have been saying goodbye...I wonder if he was already living in my future and looking back on me, sending us both a message...

The Joy And The Sorrow

"Then a woman said, 'Speak to us of joy and sorrow.' And he answered: 'Your joy is your sorrow unmasked . . . they are inseparable. Together they come, and when one sits alone with you at your board, remember that the other is asleep upon your bed.'"

Kahlil Gibran
The Prophet

Had it been only a month ago that Ted surprised me with a mystery trip to celebrate my 60th birthday? All he told me was to bring casual clothes and be ready to leave by a certain time. A pouring, drenching rain made the driving difficult as we headed south from Boston. Since I knew we had a deadline to meet, before long I guessed that we were headed for the Block Island ferry. I was excited; we had often talked about visiting this exotic little island off the coast of Connecticut. The rain was still coming down in sheets as we got off the ferry and spotted the Blue Dory. Ted told me he had selected this charming little inn because it was known as the most romantic inn on the island. It lived up to its reputation.

Ted had other surprises in mind. After arriving at our room overlooking the bay, I opened the birthday gift he'd given me and found a pair of skimpy, lacey red bikini underwear from Victoria's Secret. But then I surprised him even more by having gotten for myself an equally skimpy, lacey piece of underwear that I had promised him for his 70th birthday that had recently passed. We laughed as we imagined how <u>really</u> surprised we would have been if we had run into each other at Victoria's Secret! I'm pretty conservative as such things go, so by wearing sexy, red bikini underwear to dinner that night, I felt like a little girl dressing up in her mother's cocktail dress and high heels, or like I was putting on a Halloween costume and pretending to be a lady of the streets. It was play-acting – but such fun.

The sun streaming through our windows welcomed us to a dazzlingly beautiful, blue-skied morning, a day as inviting as the previous one had been forbidding. A perfect day for exploring. We took turns driving our rental motor scooter and tooting all over the island. We loved the island's one small village with its charming shops and cottages, the pastoral scenes of open fields and rock walls, and the towering cliffs overlooking the calm, shimmering sea. We discovered a dirt road that beckoned us, and so we left our scooter behind some trees and walked down a winding path towards the ocean. To our surprise and delight we came upon a nearly deserted, gorgeous sandy beach. We found a secluded spot behind some rocks where we could stretch out our towels and have a picnic. The sun was beating down from above and the sand and rocks reflected the heat from below and our only regret was that we hadn't packed our bathing suits. Soon the idea occurred to us: since not a soul was in sight down the long beach, why not strip down to our underwear? (We gave each other courage – alone we never would have done this.) Before long, the sun's warmth and the ocean's waves invited us to take a dip. The water was glorious; we frolicked like a couple of adolescents. As we emerged from the water, dripping wet with our underwear plastered to our skin, we found ourselves walking back to our spot on the beach alongside a man who was fully clothed – long pants, long-sleeved shirt, hat, shoes and socks. The three of us strolled along together, chatting, as if this was nothing out of the ordinary.

Later, I was a bit distressed when Ted said we had to catch the 4:00 ferry back to Boston.

"Why not stay here and have dinner? What's the hurry?" But Ted wanted to get back and have dinner there. This was peculiar. Ted was never one to keep to such a tight schedule; he was acting very strange. But as the day unfolded, Ted revealed his final surprise.

As we walked to our table at the restaurant in Cambridge, I found a group of our closest friends waiting for us. This had been a birthday of one delightful surprise after another. The really loving thing about all these surprises was that Ted hated to be surprised himself, but he knew surprises would make me happy. I remember this birthday as my happiest ever.

Ted died less than a month after our Block Island trip, and as I look back at our photographs now, I think of how innocent we were – sailing off across the water on a fun adventure to an unknown island, celebrating my birthday at that romantic little inn, riding behind Ted on our little motor scooter, lying in our underwear on the beach feeling playfully risqué. *"Your joy is your sorrow unmasked."*

When Scott arrived from Colorado for the memorial service, he wanted to see his dad one last time. He needed this to help bring him some closure since he hadn't been here when his father died. Scott and I took a trip to the mortuary. I felt like I was in a trance as we were ushered into a room that had as its centerpiece a large wooden box. And in it there he was, cold and hard, like a stone statue dressed in my husband's clothes. I hardly recognized him. I knew that his physical body was dead, but I refused to believe that his spirit had disappeared as well. Did the energy that animated that empty shell die as well? Where does the life force go after the body no longer houses it? Does it just dissipate or evaporate? Or does it maintain its integrity? As Scott and I walked out of the funeral home that day, I wondered if Ted's spirit was "out there" watching us in our pain and wanting to make it easier for us.

Then I thought of the rainbows. The horror of Ted's death followed by the sheer radiance and beauty of the rainbows – surely it had to mean something. I certainly understood that the depths of pain I was suffering spoke to the heights of joy I'd had. But then the realization dawned on me that perhaps it doesn't end there. Perhaps this horror is likewise to be followed by something profoundly good and wondrous. Perhaps the rainbows were pointing to that. It helped me to think about it that way. They spoke to the ineffable, to the mystery. A bridge to the unknown.

A short time after that, I had my first dream about Ted. He was standing there, just his normal, regular self. I was overjoyed to see him again. The message came to me that although a part of him was taken away, the essence of Ted was still alive and still with me. In the dream, there was no verbal interaction between us, just his standing there with this message. I took it to mean that his body had died, but his soul was freed and hadn't gone away. Perhaps he was reaching out to me from somewhere.

Maybe it was just my denial, my refusal to let go and accept the fact that he was dead. Denial or not, my belief that his spirit would continue on in time carried me through the dark days ahead. It gave me something to hang on to.

I had two strong, compelling desires. First, to be in touch with Ted's spirit so that I could know that he was still with me, and second, to heal myself so that I could go on and have a rich and happy life. Both seemed pretty daunting. I was clear about one thing, though. If I gave up on life I would not be honoring my husband.

Dark Nights Of The Soul

"I came home to the empty house, sick with longing."
Donald Hall
Without

Karyn stayed with me for the first two weeks as I began my new existence as a widow. Her presence helped immensely. Having her around softened the awfulness of this new life. How I dreaded that day when I would have to take her to the airport and drive back to my empty house; but that day came.

As I waved goodbye and watched her disappear into the airplane, my heart was in shreds. Emptiness faced me as I walked back to my car. For the first couple of weeks after Ted died, I'd felt wrapped in the care of others. Now, she too, like the others, had returned to her life. I was face to face with the reality that this is the way it is going to be. Alone. *What am I going to do? What is there to hang onto?* My grief felt almost beyond what the walls of my chest could contain. I finally understood what is meant by the expression "broken heart." I felt like mine was surely going to break.

As I drove past the strip mall with its gas stations and fast food restaurants, the memory of an old companion flashed through my brain. Cigarettes! Even though I had not smoked in some thirty years, it's amazing how that old crutch came to my rescue in my hour of need. I was in a horrible, *Oh, fuck it,* mood, and so I turned into the next convenience store. Feeling that nothing mattered anymore anyway, I bought a pack, and smoked them all the way home. And then I sat out on my porch and smoked some more. Sipping my hot cup of tea and inhaling the smoke deep into my lungs felt like a balm for my shredded heart. After decades of not smoking, the disgusting taste, the burning in the back of my throat and the dizziness in my head did temporarily distract me from the awfulness of my empty house and my longing.

I also felt deeply ashamed of this socially scorned behavior. If anyone had happened to drive up while I was puffing away, I would have felt mortified. In a disgusting, unhealthy way, the cigarettes got me through that first night in my house alone. Rather than feeling the raw agony of missing my husband so desperately, I found myself anxious and preoccupied with the dreaded possibility that someone might suddenly arrive and discover what an awful person I was. The cigarettes served to remove me from my pain for a while.

As I sat out on our deck in the dark looking at the stars twinkling in the vast sky, I wondered if Ted was out there anywhere. How much I wanted to believe he was with me in some form or another. I wanted him to know what I was going through. I remembered the many times in the past that Ted and I had sat out on our porch together, enjoying the night-time sky, talking about all sorts of things. Once in a great while Ted had smoked a cigar (when he wasn't in training) and I, being a former smoker, enjoyed having an occasional puff with him, disgusting as it was. Now as I sat alone on my porch with my cigarette, I felt a strange kinship with him again.

After a while, when I could not bear to smoke another one and my throat was feeling raw and sore, I gathered up my empty coffee cup and the remainder of cigarettes and went inside to face the empty house. I turned on the faucet, doused the remaining cigarettes with water, put the soggy pack in the trash compactor and smooshed it flat so that I couldn't get at them the next day. By then I'd sufficiently numbed and distracted myself enough that I could finally climb into my empty bed.

As terrible as it was to crawl into the empty bed at night, it was almost as hard to awaken in the morning greeted by his absence. My first thought was, *Maybe this is all just a bad dream.* Then the horrible reality would hit me in the face and I'd feel that sinking feeling of despair. As I was pulling up the blankets on our big, king-sized bed, I remembered the playful times Ted and I had had making this bed together. Throwing the covers up, jerking the sides straight, laughing, fluffing up the pillows, tossing them at each other.

One of these days I should wash these sheets. It's been two months now. But I don't want to wash away the last lingering odor of Ted.

Ted Rescues Me From Myself

"Someone I loved once gave me a box full of darkness.
It took me years to understand that this too, was a gift."
                                                    Mary Oliver
                                                    "When Death Comes"

On a handful of occasions in that first year without Ted, I repeated the cigarettes-on-the-porch ritual. Sometimes, when I was returning home after having been away visiting friends or family, I found it especially hard to come back to the empty house. Then I would go into my, *Oh, fuck it,* routine and head to the convenience store for some cigarettes. I'd smoke five or six, again douse the remainder with water, and throw the soggy pack into the trash compactor. Perhaps this bad-girl behavior served as an outlet for my anger at my husband for his having died on me and leaving me in such a predicament. *If I have to go it alone, at least I'll have my old buddy!* I decided I would not permit myself to indulge in this acting out beyond the first year. I didn't want to start my addiction going again.

All my reaching for cigarettes couldn't conceal how terribly I missed Ted. I think he knew it, and came to my rescue one miserable night. As I cried myself to sleep, I pleaded with Ted, *Please come to me, honey. Let me know you're still with me.*

That night I had a dream about a seemingly ordinary dog – but Ted and I were worried about her. The toes on one foot were rotting off, bit by bit. Then it came to me in the dream that a little girl, about three years old, was sadistically cutting her dog's leg off starting with the toes. A little bit at a time, she was destroying the dog's foot. What remained of the dog's front leg looked ghastly; smelly and disgusting. In my dream, I spoke sternly to the child:

"You've got to stop that! You have to take care of her."

She looked up at me and said,

"How about if we take her to the doctor?"

"That's a good idea," I said.

I think Ted sent me this dream, but not in the lovely, beautiful way I had hoped for. His message was obvious. If I didn't stop my self-destructive behavior, I would surely destroy myself. He was telling me I needed to stop medicating myself with cigarettes. Perhaps I should see a doctor (i.e., a psychotherapist) for help. I think that was the last time I smoked.

Waves Of Remembrance

"Grief is a tidal wave that overtakes you, smashes down upon you with unimaginable force, sweeping you up into its darkness, where you tumble and crash against unidentifiable surfaces, only to be thrown out on an unknown beach, bruised, reshaped."

Stephanie Ericsson
Companion Through the Darkness

A monstrous wave hit me on July 14, 2001. My Tsunami. This unleashed a succession of waves that have come, again and again. I'd be going along perfectly fine, minding my own business, when all of a sudden, the shock of an old remembrance stabbed me like a knife and loosened another wave of sadness.

One morning while I was sitting at the kitchen table – the place the two of us spent so many happy hours – I found myself frequently looking out at the street. I realized that I was watching for Ted's little blue car to come wheeling into the driveway. I was brought back with a jolt. I felt like an open, raw wound – I guess that's why they call it a "broken heart." It took nothing at all, just the tiniest thread of a memory, to set my heart bleeding. Then, all I could do was hold on and ride it out – no way of stopping it. Let those scalding hot tears rise from within me; feel them swell in my chest, my throat, and my eyes. Sometimes, the wave brimmed over and spilled out of my eyes; sometimes it stopped in my throat.

Occasionally I thought my heart might actually break, so savagely did the grief cut through me. Once when I was in such pain, with the tears pouring out my eyes and my nose dripping, I suddenly realized it was not mucous coming from my nose, but blood! I had cried so hard that I had given myself a bloody nose.

Another day, trying to be very business-like, I called the contractor who built our house.

"The world lost a big man when your husband died," he remarked.

Here they come again...my tears. Sometimes, they were unleashed when a beautiful love song that reminded me of Ted came on the radio. "The Power of Love" always got to me, as did, "Come Away with Me," "When a Man Loves a Woman," and "Lean on Me." And, of course, there's always "Amazing Grace."

I remember once when I was visiting Scott's home in Colorado, and I was sitting with his family at dinner eating pizza. I had been missing Ted and wishing he were with me. Someone said something about him that triggered a memory, and I could feel a big wave rising in my chest. I wanted to leave the table and go have a good cry. My observant ten-year-old grandson, Nathan, noticed the tears in my eyes.

"Why are you crying, Grammy?" he asked.

I explained to Nathan, "It's like sometimes when I'm feeling sad and missing Granddaddy, my tears come up all of a sudden, like a big whoosh, and I just have to wait for them to drain back down again. Which they always do."

Sometimes the waves of pain seemed not survivable. Like the pain of labor contractions, they kept coming. The intensity seemed more than I could bear. And yet, like for a pregnant woman who thinks, *The next one will surely kill me,* it does not. Ultimately she is rewarded by the birth of a most beautiful, precious little baby. One day, perhaps I will give birth to my new self.

Over time, though, I came to realize that I didn't feel bereft and anguished at every moment. I had assumed that missing Ted would be a continuous, ongoing, unrelenting way of life. I learned differently. Even in those first days, I didn't go around crying all the time. There were moments when I'd be thinking about something else. *What are we going to do about supper? I need to wash some clothes. The lawn needs to be watered. The bills need to be paid.* I was thankful that these day-to-day thoughts, having occupied my attention for even a few minutes, had allowed my sorrow to slip into the background.

A couple of weeks after Ted's death, I went to play tennis. Soon, I was caught up in the game. At one point, the thought suddenly hit me, *I'm actually having fun! I haven't thought about Ted in several minutes!* A wave of guilt swept through me, as if I'd betrayed him somehow. Was this a case of easy come, easy go? Not a chance. The full onslaught of grief was back soon enough. This was just a brief respite in the storm.

The wave-like nature of grief never failed to amaze me. I woke one morning in the early days and my tears were not around. I wondered, *Have I turned a corner?* I could walk past Ted's headband hanging on the doorknob and the poster-size picture of his face with his big radiant smile and not well up with tears. It concerned me a little. I didn't intend to be a permanently grieving widow wearing black forever, but yet I thought it was awfully self-centered of me to be able to enjoy life so soon after his death.

The next day sadness was back. Like a sledgehammer, socking me in the stomach, proving I wasn't as selfish as I'd feared. What I missed most was not having Ted to come home to at the end of the day. I could talk to him about anything. He was my anchor, my shelter in the storm. I could count on his accepting and loving me no matter what embarrassing thing I had to share. He could fix anything: my bicycle, my necklace, my computer; he could also tend to my wounded feelings and shaken self-confidence. *Where are you now, Ted, to fix my broken heart?* So often I had wanted to tell him about what I was going through and how I was trying to be brave. I wanted him to hold me and say, "You're doing a good job, honey. Just hang in there."

I wished I could get some sign from him that he was with me. Then, one night, I saw it... a huge, gorgeous double rainbow. It stretched across the entire sky from horizon to horizon. Was that a sign?

What Was It Like For You To Die?

So often I've been drawn back to wondering what it was like for Ted when he died. I have tried to reconstruct those final moments of his life. He was, quite literally, rowing his heart out, giving it his all in a race that was twice as long as he had expected. His boat crossed the finish line. And then what happened?

Did he feel more than the usual pain and exhaustion after rowing a hard race? Did his heart monitor (which he always wore to help him stay within the safe limits of exercise) signal him that he was in trouble? As awful as it might have been, I wish I could know what he went through that day. Doctors say that he probably died of ventricular fibrillation. (However, the autopsy listed the official cause of death as "fresh water drowning" because fibrillation doesn't show up on an autopsy.) Sometimes I wonder if he was just so exhausted that he simply passed out, or perhaps his energy was so depleted that he didn't have the strength to maintain the control to keep his boat upright. These long, narrow racing shells overturn easily if a rower doesn't keep his body centrally positioned in the boat with both oars perfectly balanced on the water. It's possible, I thought, that Ted may have collapsed or fainted, and that his boat flipped over and trapped him under water with his feet still strapped to his boat. I'm haunted by terrible images of what might have been his last moments. I imagine his panic...water flooding his throat and lungs...thrashing, struggling to get free, not able to breathe, desperately wanting help to come. Or did he simply lose consciousness and slip away? Were his last moments ones of terror or grace?

So often I have wondered what his experience of dying was like. Did the realization come to him that he was going to die? I wonder if he regretted having made rowing so important (my anger again). I would like to think his last thoughts were about me and the children. I've read accounts of Near Death Experiences and wonder if he experienced going down a long, dark tunnel towards a brilliant white light with a loving person to greet him and help him cross over. For Ted that day, however, no one told him to go back – it _was_ his time.

At the time I was completely oblivious to all of this. I had just been going about my day, not knowing that Ted's life, and mine as I had known it, was ending. I would like to be able to say that, because of our loving connection to each other, I'd had some kind of a knowing, a premonition that something cataclysmic was happening. One often hears of such stories...of a sudden vision coming at the exact time a loved one was dying. But I was probably buying lettuce and picking out tomatoes at the local farm stand when all this was happening to my husband.

I suppose it's natural to feel some guilt when a loved one dies, as if our presence could have made the difference. I've thought that maybe, if I'd been there, the day would have turned out differently. Maybe he wouldn't have pushed himself so hard. Maybe I could have swum out to help him – which, of course, is ridiculous.

I'm not superwoman; I cannot leap tall buildings in a single bound or swim a quarter of a mile in no time flat. I can't even *swim* a quarter of a mile.

As horrific as it would've been, I wish I had been there with my husband. I just assumed that when that fateful day came, I would have been by his side, holding his hand, going as far as I could with him on his final journey. My heart breaks thinking of him all alone out on the water as he faced his dying.

When Ted was living, he thought a lot about death, a subject that fascinated him. Many of his writings in his last few years reflected his curiosity about death. He wondered, "What is it like to die?"

Several years earlier, Ted had an amazing experience that helped answer his question. He found it comforting then, and it comforts me now.

On that beautiful fall weekend six years earlier, Ted and I had attended an experiential eco-psychology conference at a retreat center in rural, western Massachusetts. We both were interested in learning how to use nature as a healing tool in working with our patients. As therapists, we often learned a new psychotherapy modality by first experiencing it personally and applying it to our own life concerns. It was a Saturday night, and we had spent a long, emotionally intense day with our group participating in various exercises, including some deep, rapid breathing exercises. Then we each lay down on the floor on our mats and focused on our own personal issues.

Ted wrote the following account of his experience:

"*The room was filled with breathing. In and out as deeply and rapidly as possible. I was lying there observing it all, unmoved by the experience. Some were crying, yelling, holding each other, and some, like me were apparently unmoved. I began to remember my father on his deathbed. After staying with that vision for a while, I became aware that I too would be dying soon, and that my father would not be able to see me go through that process, because he was gone. Nor would I be able to witness the deaths of my children, since I wouldn't be there. I began to think about my own death and I suddenly became frightened. I missed my father terribly. He had always been there for me in the major transitions in my life, marriages, deaths, births, graduations, and I wished now that he would be there to comfort and steady me at the hour of my death. This would be the most important moment in my life. I needed him to tell me how to do it. I realized I was alone now, and he couldn't tell me what I wanted, hold my hand, or, as was his custom, to hold my gaze. I was frightened and alone. I felt like a four-year-old in full panic. After a while Jennifer (one of the facilitators) put my head in her lap and we breathed together. Someone put a pillow under my knees, and Jennifer put a pillow under my head and I was quiet and relaxed. Then she left. This is what it's like to die, I thought. They hold your hand, then they make you comfortable and then they leave. I am alone at the moment of death. After a while longer I began to think of my mother who died. She could not tell me how to die, and could not comfort me as I thought about my own death. Then I thought of Judy who also had died without telling me what she knew, except to lean forward and kiss me. Perhaps there was a message in that.*

After a while I decided to get up, slowly, so as not to fall over, and go outside into the cold night. I was barefoot, the grass was wet, and the wind was blowing. The sky was dark except for a full moon and occasional wisps of clouds, each of which showed up as a fuzzy black blotch surrounded by a silvery border, setting it off from the black sky. I looked up through the naked branches of the trees and saw a small cloud passing in front of the full moon. I said to myself, this is the moment of my death. When the moon goes out I shall die. The cloud was not large enough to completely obliterate the moon, which continued to shine faintly through the cloud's blackness. I said to myself, that was a dress rehearsal. And surely, the small cloud soon brought behind it a larger one, quite dense enough to do the job. I was aware of the intensely glorious night, the crispness of the night, the wind blowing through my shirt, the wetness of the grass on my toes, my physical body which by now was reaching with out-stretched arms to take it all in; the beauty of the world, the magnificence of existence, the inner experience of joy, the clarity of perception. The stark branches of the sleeping tree, the vastness of the distant moon, the intervening clouds reminding me of the reality of atmosphere plasma.

Suddenly I knew the message from my father, my mother and from Judy. They were telling me that death is not a problem, but a celebration of life that itself is ecstasy. To be conscious and alive is such an ecstatic experience, and dying is just a way of capping it and acknowledging that. When the time comes for you, go with gratitude, love and joy, celebrate your life, and teach that to your children.

After that a wave of contentment came over me. I became aware of a sensation of a band around my right wrist. I thought I had a bracelet on and kept looking down at the wrist and rubbing it to locate the source of the feeling. I realized that it was a hospital bracelet I had worn when I was having my dress rehearsal of dying in 1984 (when he'd nearly died from a serious blood disease). *No, I thought, it is the bracelet I now wear daily. We are all dying and cannot take off our bracelets. I just don't notice it most of the time. So it is for all of us. Not one of us gets out of here alive. We are too scared to notice the beauty of life, and we miss the celebration of that. To not pass this on to others is to conspire with the fear. I cannot do my own life justice, cannot live fully if those around me are not fully living. I will try to keep our dying in front of those I love, in order to fully live, connected through life with others."*

Then it all became clear to me! Ted wrote about wanting his father to tell him how to die and to be with him and comfort him at this most important moment of his life. I truly believe now that Ted sent the rainbows as his way of telling us what it is like to die. He wanted to tell us what he'd hoped to learn from his father. Just as he received the message that night from the clouds, the moon, the glorious night, I believe the rainbows were his way of telling us, *"Death is not a problem...To be conscious and alive is such an ecstatic experience, and death is just a way of capping it."*

And maybe his father was there after all, helping him to cross over to the other side.

The First Thanksgiving – A Lesson Learned

"The presence of that absence is everywhere."
Edna St. Vincent Millay
Savage Beauty: the Life of Edna St. Vincent Millay

What was I going to do for my first Thanksgiving without Ted? I dreaded it. I decided a change in routine might make it less painful, so I took myself off to Colorado, to my son Scott's home. There I could get caught up in the happy whirlwind of his family's busy life and, for a few days, forget my loneliness. Playing with my two adorable grandsons, Nathan and Kenny, and helping my daughter-in-law Debbie with preparations for an over-the-top, magnificent Thanksgiving dinner was going to be a welcome distraction from the awfulness of the first holiday without Ted. I thought it was just what I needed.

The lavishly decorated table was laden with platters of turkey and dressing, steaming bowls of sweet potatoes, broccoli and green beans, squash, mashed potatoes and gravy, baskets of hot rolls and pumpkin bread, cranberries, and relish. I looked around the table at my family and our long-time good friends who had joined us. It was a picture-perfect family gathering – but I felt numb. The conversation at dinner swirled around me as I sat with a frozen look of pleasantness on my face. Now and then, I uttered little social niceties that seemed appropriate to the conversation, which was about everything except the fact that Ted wasn't with us.

By and by these friends left, but were soon replaced by another couple who came for dessert. I didn't know these people at all, and I found it hard to maintain my mask of politeness. The last thing I wanted to do was smile and make nice to these people who did little more than acknowledge Ted's death when they were introduced to me. I couldn't stand this charade for one more minute. The feeling suddenly came over me, *I've got to get out of here.*

Making a rather lame excuse, I announced, "I'm going outside to get a little air." I put on my coat and walked out the door. Without a destination, I walked down the street and then wandered up a hillside to a spot where I could sit and be alone. And then the tears came. Nothing stopping them now. I sobbed and sobbed. Finally I could be real. Tears of guilt and self-recrimination replaced tears of sadness. I felt so angry that we hadn't even once acknowledged Ted during this first Thanksgiving dinner without him. How could I have let this happen? I imagined him out there in the stars somewhere wondering if we'd forgotten him already. I felt horrible. I knew Scott and Debbie and our friends were just trying to get through this horribly difficult first Thanksgiving without Ted. They didn't want to make me sad by talking about Ted. But I was already sad beyond belief, and acknowledging our missing Ted wasn't going to make me feel any worse. Sharing our sadness would at least help us feel closer to each other, whereas not talking about Ted and having to "make nice" left us each isolated in our grief.

I learned the hard way that I needed to make sure Ted would be a part of all our family holidays and celebrations in the future, because that would keep his spirit alive and present with us, and would make me feel less alone. I emerged from the Thanksgiving ordeal better prepared to face Christmas.

I began a tradition that I continue to this day. Whenever we have a family get-together for some celebratory occasion, after we're all gathered around the table and before we begin to eat, I light a special candle for granddaddy. We have a moment or two of silence as we bring Ted's spirit more consciously into our circle.

Several years later at one of our family occasions, something unexpected happened. As I lit the granddaddy candle, I spoke to Skyler and Ian, who hadn't yet been born when Ted died.

"It's too bad you never knew your granddaddy."

Five-year-old Skye piped up.

"We _know_ him, we just never _met_ him."

Worse Than My Worst Imaginings

"Worrying does not empty tomorrow of its troubles
It empties today of its strength."

Corrie Ten Bloom
Clippings from my Notebook

Occasionally, I'd let the thought enter my head that, because of our ten-year age difference, Ted would probably die first. This would be horrible, so I hadn't let myself go far into that dreaded reality. Yet, it stayed in the back of my mind. Ted and I had talked about one or the other of us dying "someday." Of course, this "someday" was always way off in the distant, non-existent future.

At other times, Ted joked about it.

"I get to go first next time."

He had already gone through the devastating loss of his first wife, who died unexpectedly when their twins were only five years old. He never wanted to endure such pain again. I expected that, at some point, I'd be facing this myself. I just didn't know when or how. Some people go through a long, slow, agonizing descent toward death, whereas others are taken away suddenly at the height of their vitality. Would something catastrophic erupt: a stroke, a heart attack, or an accident? Ted had often said he liked leaving things when he was at the top of his game. He had left his position as Assistant Commissioner of Mental Health when he was at his peak. He fully retired from his psychotherapy practice when it was thriving. He pushed us to sell our beach home soon after we'd gotten it up and running and he'd completed all his projects. Ted was not one for lying in a hammock, watching the clouds go by and just getting old. So, perhaps it's not surprising that he left the world when he was strong, vital and full of life.

Some of my anxiety was realistic. After all, he had always liked to take risks. He had flown airplanes, enjoyed white water canoeing, and even done some hang gliding many years ago. (Indeed, we'd done these things together.) He enjoyed winter camping and backpacking trips. Recently he'd been further pushing his limits by learning to ice climb. The previous winter, at 69 years of age, he decided he wanted to learn to snowboard. When he went off on a climbing trip, I'd worry about him if I didn't hear from him at the time he said he'd be off the mountain. I worried that he'd fall to his death on the rocks, that his crampons would fail to hold while ice climbing. I worried that he would he fall asleep and drive off the road.

I knew some of my anxiety about his dying was neurotic, a carry-over from my childhood anxiety that something terrible and unpredictable might happen to the man I loved. Growing up with my father's alcoholism left me fearful that his erratic behavior would turn my life upside down. I was always alert to something unpredictable happening: "hyper-vigilant" is the term used for this in psychotherapy.

I worked throughout our marriage to free myself of this neurotic anxiety, and not to put onto Ted the expectation that he would suddenly devastate me as my father had. And I was largely successful at it. When a sense of alarm rose in my chest if Ted didn't come home at the expected time, I could usually convince myself that the fear was "old stuff," and not give voice to it. I didn't want to put a damper on his enthusiasm by being an old nag, a worrywart.

Ironically, I did not worry much about Ted's rowing. The message, of course, is that it's pointless to worry about things you have no control over – something else is going to get you in the end anyway.

In spite of all my anxiety, when the fateful call came, I was blind-sided. Here with me one moment, happy and sparkling with life, and just two hours later dead, completely dead. *Couldn't he be just partially dead? Or dead for just a little while?* A kind of panic set in. I felt desperate and frantic to bring my husband back. Of course, the realization would soon hit me in the face once again; it is hopeless, he really is gone. And then, talk about despair....

In the crises I've faced over my lifetime – my father's alcoholism, financial worries, challenges in raising adolescents – there was always something I, or we, could do about them. With effort – sometimes considerable – we could turn these situations around. Studying and achieving in school, working harder to earn more money, attending therapy and self-help groups had in the past served to reverse the tides of disaster. I'm a person who likes to fix things rather than accepting an unhappy outcome. But there was no fixing this one.

Nor was I prepared for this degree of sorrow and anguish. My sister had died a couple of years earlier, my mother four years before that, and my father some twenty years earlier. Yet, all of these deaths came after years of increasing disability, and although at the time I felt great sadness, I grieved these family members more at a distance. I still could get up in the morning, go to work, do the laundry, drive the kids to their soccer games and swim practice, make love with my husband. I dealt with the loss of my mother, father and sister alongside these daily events. As I was moving along through my day, I'd occasionally be brought up short by the sudden realization, *My mother is dead; I can't just pick up the phone and hear her voice.* After getting word that my father had died, I had even been able to attend a banquet and lecture that evening before getting on a plane the next day to fly to his funeral in Denver.

Grief for my husband was different. He was life itself. I felt my life was over, too.

When the death of my husband was still just a hypothetical possibility, I didn't have any real idea of what I was in for. The only experience I had to draw upon was going to friends' funerals and watching other widows. My attention was focused on helping my friends through those first few days – their having to hear the dreadful news, the gathering of relatives and friends and then the funeral itself. I had imagined that getting through the memorial or funeral would be the hardest part. I wondered how I would ever have held up if I'd been in their shoes. Would I have been able to keep myself together during the service? Would I have been able to greet the guests in the receiving line? I anticipated that the empty house after the children left would be hard. But I assumed that soon after, the healing would begin.

In fact, during my first days as a widow, I was in shock. My psyche came to my rescue by wrapping me in a protective cocoon of numbness. I was surrounded by the love and care of friends and family. Further, the rituals of notifying people, writing the obituary, planning the memorial service, picking out the urn, arranging appointments with lawyers, all had left me with little time to feel. It was only later, long after the memorial service, after all had gone back to their busy lives and these protective layers had receded that I began to feel the devastation. Then, the full onslaught of grief obliterated my senses.

As Joan Didion writes:

"The difference between grief as we imagine it
and grief as it is, is the unending absence that follows...
the void...the relentless succession of moments during which we will confront the
experience of meaninglessness itself."

That unending absence is what I found the hardest; that repeated realization that he was gone.

He is gone.

A Cinderella Story

Shortly after Ted died, I heard a phrase, "Memories are in the details." This gave me the idea of writing the story of my life with Ted. I knew that, in time, the details of our life together would fade, and I'd wanted to grab hold of these memories while they were still clear in my mind.

I decided to be as open and candid as possible within the limits of what I would be comfortable having my children and ancestors read someday. I gathered together old calendars and appointment books and pored through photo albums that I had assembled over the years in order to help myself remember what we had done in our 35 years together. Tucked away in the back of my bureau drawer, I came across a stack of birthday, anniversary and Valentine's Day cards that Ted had given me in the past. (How glad I am that I had saved these!) Then, I wove together my written story together with these cards and photographs.

I followed the story through all the events of our lives together, trying as authentically as possible to represent the reality of our lives as a couple, and in the family we created. I didn't want to write some idealized, glossed-over version of our marriage.

As I re-lived the joys and adventures as well as some of the struggles and challenges we had faced, I found the process of telling the story tremendously healing. I laughed, I cried and I felt enormously grateful for my good fortune in having had Ted as my husband. I thought, if I ever developed Alzheimer's and lost my mind, I could pick up this book and remind myself, *There once was a man who dearly loved me.*

I began our story at the beginning.

My marriage to Ted was a Cinderella tale. I was just a young thing – naïve, unsophisticated, and inexperienced – back in 1966 when I met Ted. I had grown up in Colorado and had attended both college and graduate school there. This had given me enough courage and confidence – what I call "escape velocity" – to leave home. I moved to California and had been living with a friend in a three-room apartment and working at my first job as a clinical social worker.

One day, as I walked out of the lunchroom of the San Mateo Department of Health and Welfare where I worked, a tall, lanky, ruggedly handsome man with a boyish grin walked up to me in the hallway.

"Hi, you don't know who I am. I'm Ted Anderson. I've been wanting to ask you out – would you like to go to a movie Saturday night?"

I was completely taken aback, but intrigued, and without knowing more about him other than his name, I said yes. We worked the arrangements out, and I walked back to my office and told my secretary.

"Say, this Ted Anderson just asked me out."

"Oh," she exclaimed, "Ted Anderson! He's that nice psychiatrist whose wife just died, and he has two adorable little twins. And, he drives a red Porsche!"

I was excited when Ted came to pick me up. As we walked into the movies, he spoke to me. "This is the first date I've been on in ten years – I guess I'm supposed to ask if you'd like some popcorn?"

Ted's disarming and unpretentious manner made me feel comfortable. Somewhere in the middle of the movie, we agreed we would rather get to know each other than watch the movie, and we left. We talked for hours in a little cocktail lounge discovering how much we had in common, besides the similarity of our professions. Among them was a love of Colorado. Ted had interned at the Denver General Hospital, had skied the same slopes as I'd learned to ski on, and had a good friend who owned a ranch in the Blue River valley not far from my grandparents' ranch. By the time I went back to my apartment, I was smitten.

My first words to my roommate as I walked in the door were, "I'd marry that guy in a minute." It was magical. I had dated a lot of men before meeting Ted and had never felt this way about anyone. He was in a different league. I had met my Prince Charming.

Although we both worked at the same mental health center, I had never noticed Ted before that day. As it turned out, our meeting wasn't quite as random as it seemed to me at the time. Later, I learned that he'd had his eye on me for quite a while, and had finally gotten up his courage to ask me out. He had orchestrated the timing so that when I walked out one door of the cafeteria, he had left through the other door, arranging it so that we both arrived in the outer hallway at the same time. Six months earlier, Ted's first wife had died of a rare form of acute asthma. He was just beginning the quest to find a wife and a mother for his five-year-old twins.

For each of us in our own ways, dating each other was a huge risk. For me, Ted was a stretch – ten years older, a father of two children, a well-established psychiatrist who was highly thought of in the community and living in a beautiful contemporary home in the San Mateo highlands. Ted, meanwhile, had a lot riding on finding the right woman. She needed to have the potential to be a loving mother, to be able to hold her own socially in his group of similarly successful, sophisticated professionals; she had to be able to be independent and take care of herself, and also be able to share his love of the outdoors and venturing into the unknown.

My handsome prince put me through many tests. He needed to make sure the shoe would fit. On our second date, Ted invited me up to his home for a hamburger cookout and to meet Scott and Sandy. The three of them came to pick me up at my apartment in Ted's old VW camper. I was struck by how tall they were. Not having had much experience with 5-year-olds, I had pictured little children. I think they were as afraid of me as I was of them, because as soon as we got into the camper they immediately retreated to the rear of the van, where they remained for the remainder of the trip. (These were the days before seat belts.) After dinner, I went off to play with the children while Ted cleaned up the kitchen. Sandy and I played dolls in her bedroom. She was easy to be with and seemed starved for female attention. I enjoyed noticing Ted peek his head around the corner and smile at us playing on the floor. Scott was more shy and reticent, but later the four of us played with his trains on the big track Ted had made in his bedroom.

Having assessed my "potential to be a good mother" criteria, Ted tested my courage and spirit of adventure. On our third date, he invited me to go camping with him and his children for the weekend in the high Sierras. Enjoying this kind of adventure and being a bit of a risk taker, I said sure. (The risk was not about camping in the mountains, but about sleeping next to a man I hardly knew in a VW van on my third date! I grew up in the 1950's, and we didn't do that sort of thing back then.) I thought, *Wow, this is moving ahead fast!* But I trusted my instincts.

The four of us left Friday night after work and drove eastward from San Francisco for about three hours. By the time we reached the mountains, it was late. Ted's old camper could barely manage the rocky, four-wheel-drive road. In order to make it up the last steep incline, he slipped the clutch, lurched forward, re-started the engine, slipped the clutch and lurched forward another few feet and kept repeating

this maneuver until we arrived at a level place where we could spend the night. Harrowing, but fun.

Then I faced another challenge – getting ready for bed. Ted said he would take a little walk while I changed. Sandy and Scott were all eyes as I tried to act like this was no big deal and nonchalantly pulled off my jeans and shirt, unhooked my bra and pulled on my pajamas. Then Ted returned to the camper and crawled into his sleeping bag beside mine. I don't even remember if we gave each other a goodnight kiss.

I wouldn't say that Ted was consciously trying to test me. He was simply introducing me to his life. He loved the outdoors and the challenge of new adventures, and he wanted someone he could share them with, along with his children. Two years later the handsome prince

Our 30th Wedding Anniversary

and Cinderella were married and they lived happily ever after. Or at least for the next 33 years until, one day, my coach turned into a pumpkin.

I look back now at photographs of us – smiling, happy and blissfully unaware of what was in store for us. How unsuspecting we were. It is good we don't know what heartaches might be waiting for us down the road. We need to bring our innocence and freshness to life.

And now, forty years later, the prince's widow is the one who is trying shoes on potential romantic partners. Ironically, in a recent dream, there was a scene revolving around Ted's size 13 shoes.

It seems there was a big problem with the shoes: no one could be found who could wear them! I don't need a psychoanalyst to interpret that one.

Back To Work

"We give comfort and receive comfort, sometimes at the same time."
Unknown

I went back to work only a week after Ted died. Now I had to support myself. I couldn't rely on Ted to take care of me. I didn't take more time off because I felt financially precarious. This probably was more a reflection of my new sense of fragility and vulnerability than my actual financial situation.

Over the years, Ted and I had regularly contributed to our joint retirement account; however, for whatever reason, he had decided not to invest in life insurance. To do so, he felt, would be to jinx himself in his risky life style. He somehow thought that if he didn't have any insurance, nothing bad would ever happen to him. No matter how many times my financial advisor reassured me that I had enough money, I never felt secure. *Enough* was a long ways from *ample* in my mind.

In addition, I went back to work so soon because I needed the structure of somewhere to go each day. I was helped enormously by feeling I was making a difference in other people's lives rather than rattling around in my empty house feeling sorry for myself. Still, on that first day back, I felt like a life-size, wind-up mannequin. I was merely going through the motions as I walked up the long flight of stairs to my office, turned the key in my door, switched on the lights and took out the files of the clients I'd be seeing. As I greeted my first client I wondered, *Is this what is meant by "The Walking Dead?"* I certainly felt like something had died inside of me since I had last been in this office. Yet, here I was, supposedly carrying on like normal. Most of my clients had been told that there had been a "death in the family" when my friend had called to cancel their appointments.

A week later when I sat with my clients for the first time, the reason for my absence was the main issue before us. I thought it was important to acknowledge that it was my husband who had died, rather than leave it vague. Otherwise, it would have been the proverbial elephant in the room.

My first client looked nonplused. My personal life had intruded itself into her therapy, and she didn't know what to do with this information. She couldn't just be oblivious to me as a person, so she voiced some perfunctory words.

"I'm sorry to hear about your husband's death…"

Then we quickly picked up where she'd left off two weeks before.

Another said:

"How can I talk about my five-year-old who's misbehaving when you've just lost your husband? My problems are so minor!"

I assured her that my personal loss didn't diminish the importance of what she was going through.

And then there were the many clients who responded with heartfelt concern and warmth. One woman smiled kindly and said:

"I feel so sad for what you're going through."

I dissolved in a rush of tears. Seeing my eyes fill up she apologized, but I assured her that she didn't make me cry.

"My tears just come to the surface at certain moments when kindness reaches out," I said, as I thanked her for her concern. I was then able to be available to this client again.

"Now let's go back to you. How are you?"

I know my clients were relieved when they saw that I was not going to burden them with my grief. I also felt glad to discover that I was able to set aside my own sadness and put my full attention on them and listen to their stories. In fact, I found that I was able to be *more* empathic with *their* suffering, especially when they were dealing with sadness and loss.

Still, there were times when listening to a couple bicker about whose turn it was to do the laundry or take out the trash, I felt like saying, *Oh, for heaven's sake, knock it off! Stop fighting and start appreciating each other – it's later than you think!* Of course, I restrained myself and recognized this impulse as an intrusion of my own grief and anger into their therapy. Then, I could go back to being present with them again. The hours that passed with my clients provided a welcome respite.

But at the end of each day, as I closed my office door and walked out into the world, the reality that "My husband is dead" would once again slam me in the face. Many a night I'd sob all the way to my car. The tears I'd been largely holding at bay all day could finally have their release.

My Mirror Is Shattered

"Sometimes I think I have touched the bottom of despair
And I can't go farther,
And I go farther."

Unknown

Several years after Ted's death, I went to the theater. It was a delightful play, a poignant love story, and I came home a wreck. A scene in the play of a tall handsome man dancing with his beautiful wife sent me into a tailspin. Sweet memories of swing dancing with my husband flooded me. I can't say we were wonderful dancers, but we had enjoyed a few lessons and had come to love swing dancing. I was taken back to the last time we danced – at Ted's 50th Harvard reunion party. Oh how we danced – we flowed, coming together, coming apart, twirling, spinning and turning. I always felt held by his eyes; seeing his joy and love reflected in his eyes. I loved feeling his tall, strong body, his arms encircling me and holding me tightly, and his face next to mine. I felt cherished. And I know that's how he felt.

The part of me that was able to feel a welling up of romantic tenderness, the part of me that could dance with such exquisite joy, had vanished. To be sure, I could still express tenderness and feel joy as I held my precious little grandchildren in my lap – and I dearly loved to do this. But I missed holding my husband in my arms.

In the first years after Ted died, I felt smaller, weaker and less substantial as a person. I believed I had lost the most vital part of myself. What was left seemed broken, insufficient. Over the years, being married to Ted had amplified me. Marriage made me more than myself. Because he loved me, he reflected back a larger, fuller version of myself. Within our marriage, I began seeing myself through his eyes, and somehow I felt more believable to myself. This had taken place gradually over time, without my even realizing it.

For example, on the dance floor, I'd gone from feeling awkward and self-conscious in my early years to feeling full of joy, energy and life. I'd become totally caught up in the music, oblivious and relaxed about how I looked.

One of Ted's patients (who continued her psychotherapy with me after Ted died) once observed Ted looking at me from across the waiting room in our office. She saw the love and pride reflected in his face, and the resulting subtle change in his posture. As she put it, "The sight of you made him proud. He stood up straighter and puffed out a bit." The sense of expansiveness she had noticed worked both ways for Ted and me.

Ted's dying took away not only our loving relationship, but also my seeing myself through his eyes as a loving and lovable woman. Ted used to say, *"You get more beautiful the older you get"* – and I felt beautiful. When I looked into the mirror of my husband's eyes, I saw a beautiful woman. After he died, when I looked into the mirror, I saw wrinkles and blemishes, tired eyes and thinning hair. Where did that beautiful woman go? Ted's dying not only took away his love, but it shattered the mirror that reflected my own sense of lovability back to myself. It worked the other way too. When I looked at Ted, I still saw the tall, ruggedly handsome man I'd fallen in love with 35 years ago. I know my behavior toward him reflected that. Sometimes, if I stepped back and looked at him "objectively," he looked old to me – he did have a lot of creases and wrinkles. But hearts have a clearer vision than eyes.

Not only do we see a reflection of ourselves when we receive love, but also – and this is even more important – when we _give_ love. When I touched or spoke to Ted in a loving way, my own loving nature was reflected back to me. Love needs an object in order to see itself. When I expressed my love to Ted, he acted as a mirror for that place within me that is able to love. That was how I could connect with that part of myself. It's like a series of reflecting mirrors. Loving and being loved mirrors and intensifies each other's sense of lovability. When I lost Ted, when my mirror was shattered, I lost my connection with that loving place within myself.

Two days after that painful memory of our dancing, I had a marvelous dream of Ted. In the dream, I was swinging from the end of a long rope that connected high up to the sky and disappeared into somewhere unknown. I swung back and forth, going down and up, higher and higher, soaring again and again, high up into the sky. And each time that I came down, I'd push off with my feet, like you would push off of a trampoline, and then I would soar up high again. It went on and on, as I kept making myself go higher and higher. I felt like a bird, free. I was flying. In my dream it was clear that I was able to do this because of Ted. He was the wind beneath my wings. I was connected to something beyond.

I could only trust that, someday, I would rediscover those essential aspects of myself that were lost when Ted died. That's what the dream hinted at. My experience of holding the rope, pushing off and soaring was similar to my memories of dancing the swing with Ted. The only difference was that my partner couldn't be seen. He was there, but invisible. The dream told me that I am still connected to Ted's spirit. He is no longer in the world of form. The promise is that, if I do my part (in the dream I had to push off with my feet), I will heal from my sorrow and I will discover a connection with him spiritually, in the formless, and then I will rediscover joy, freedom and love within myself.

Heart Beats

"That which does not kill me makes me stronger."
Friedrich Nietzsche
Twilight of the Idols and Anti-Christ

Several months after Ted died, as I was coming home from work, I turned into the driveway and noticed that the grass was once again long and shaggy. I was exhausted. I'd been burning the candle at both ends – up at 5:30 am and not getting to bed until nearly midnight every day – keeping myself going on large amounts of caffeine. I'd been looking forward to putting my feet up, but I guessed my day wasn't over yet.

So I wheeled the old mower out of the shed, checked the oil level like I remember Ted doing, filled the tank with gasoline and pulled on the cord. Nothing. I yanked the cord again and again, each pull liberally spiced with some *"god damnits; Why did you have to leave me with this mess to deal with, Ted!"* Finally the old machine sputtered to life. That was the hardest part. When Ted was living, he used to start the mower and snow blower and I did the walking. We had a nice division of labor. He had the muscles and I had the legs.

A couple of hours later, I'd finished the job and went in to enjoy the rest of the evening. I reheated some food left over from the night before, poured myself a glass of wine, and sat down with a stack of bills to pay. In the background, a mindless TV program was on ready to be watched – Desperate Housewives (they think *they* are desperate?). As I sat there watching the images flickering on the screen, I began to be aware of a fluttering in my chest. At first, I didn't pay any attention to it – just a background sensation – but as I became more aware of the sensations, a ripple of uneasiness ran through my mind. Something was going on. When I finally got up the nerve to put my finger on my inner wrist and try to measure what my pulse rate was, I became alarmed. My heart was thumping so fast I couldn't even count it and it was jumping all around.

A rush of panic swept through my body. Something was clearly wrong. What should I do? By now it was 10:30 at night, and I didn't feel safe going to bed in this state. It never occurred to me to pick up the phone and call a friend. So I decided I should drive to the ER. Calling 911 and having an ambulance and perhaps a fire engine arrive in my driveway with flashing lights and sirens was certainly ridiculous. I felt perfectly fine.

As I drove down the dark, empty streets, my mind kept trying to make sense of this bizarre situation. *This is silly, there's nothing wrong with you...but something is going on. I wonder if you are having a heart attack... It's probably nothing, you're just tired; you should turn around and go home.* But the sheer momentum of driving, unimpeded by traffic or stoplights, kept me moving along. Before I could act on my ambivalence, I had arrived at Lahey Clinic's Emergency Room.

The waiting room was so packed that I nearly turned around. This was silly, I told myself again. I was not having an emergency. I thought, *Well, I'm here now and might as well tell someone what's going on.* I reported to the woman behind the counter that my pulse seemed to be very fast and irregular. To my surprise, rather than telling me to take a seat and wait my turn, the nurse immediately had me come to an exam room, and clamped a little device on my forefinger that registered my pulse rate.

"You are in atrial fibrillation," she announced. I was stunned.

Holy shit, what's that? I wondered. The word fibrillation sent thoughts of Ted flashing through my mind. Before I knew it, she'd returned pushing a wheel chair, told me to sit in it and wheeled me off to an even bigger room with all kinds of devices and instruments with tubes and dials. As I lay there on the examination bed, I felt like I was in some bizarre movie. Now I was getting alarmed. They must think something serious is going on if they wouldn't even let me walk by myself the 30 feet down the hall. The nurse hooked me up to a heart monitor and an IV tube and stuck an oxygen tube in my nose.

I thought that maybe I wasn't seeing the whole picture. I wondered if some mysterious process was at work, conspiring to bring Ted and me together even in our demise. I remembered reading somewhere that, after a death, the spouse often develops symptoms similar to those that the loved one died from. Ted died of ventricular fibrillation; how ironic that now I am in atrial fibrillation. As I lay there, I also remembered what I had read in Joan Didion's book, *The Year of Magical Thinking.* There is a high incidence of heart attacks and death in the first year after a spouse dies.

I also read that Holmes and Rahe had developed a Stress Scale that measures the degree of stress for various life events. Out of 43 stressful life events, death of a spouse is life's <u>most</u> stressful event. It is also correlated with an increased risk of illness.

The doctor and nurses tried several things to get my pulse regulated but to no avail. Finally they said they were going to admit me overnight.

That night, I had a frightening dream.

I was in a car with Ted, who was driving. I was sitting in the passenger seat. Our car was plunging straight down a long, steep hill, going faster and faster, out of control. Ted admitted that he'd gotten distracted and allowed this to happen (his old ADD!) I was scared. We got going so fast our car left the road and was flying through the air. Terrifying. But just before we hit the fence, Ted finally landed the car safely in a field. The message was clear. I've got to slow down and take control of my life before some disaster happens.

Twenty-four hours later, I was back home again, my heart having decided to behave itself. But now I was armed with new marching orders for the future: beta-blocker pills to take twice a day, plus the advice to lower or eliminate my intake of caffeine and not to push myself so hard. I also decided it was time to hire someone to cut my lawn in the summer and snow-blow my driveway in the winter. I didn't have to do it all.

Part II.
GOING ON

"Before you know what kindness really is
you must lose things,
feel the future dissolve in a moment
like salt in a weakened broth.
What you held in your hand,
what you counted and carefully saved,
all this must go so you know
how desolate the landscape can be
between regions of kindness.

How you ride and ride
thinking the bus will never stop.
The passengers eating maize and chicken
will stare out the window forever.

Before you learn the tender gravity of kindness,
you must travel where the Indian in the white poncho
lies dead by the side of the road.
You must see how this could be you,
how he was someone
who jouneyed through the night with plans
and the simple breath that kept him alive.

Before you know kindness as the deepest thing inside,
you must know sorrow as the other deepest thing.
You must wake up with sorrow,
you must speak to it till your voice
catches the thread of all sorrows
and you see the size of the cloth.

Then it is only kindness that makes sense anymore,
only kindness that ties your shoes
and sends you out into the day to mail letters and purchase bread.
Only kindness that raises its head
from the crowd of the world to say
it is I you have been looking for,
and then goes with you everywhere
like a shadow or a friend."

Naomi Shahib Nye
"Kindness", *Words Under the Words: Selected Poems*

Just Put One Foot In Front of The Other

"When time has stolen away our stars
and only the night endures,
somewhere in the darkness, my love,
my hand will still seek yours.

When youth has danced its parting dance
And tasted its last sweet wine,
Somewhere in the silence, my love,
your hand will still find mine."

Adele Sanborn

Why did I agree to do this? I wondered as I stumbled through the darkness. The rain fell steadily, making the walking slippery and treacherous. I stumbled over tree roots snaking their way across the path, and slipped on jutting rocks. My arms, each weighed down with cumbersome duffle bags, were unable to adjust the headlamp that kept slipping off my forehead into my eyes.

It was only two months after Ted had died, and my friend had invited me to join her and a group of friends for Labor Day weekend at Three-Mile Island, a rustic Appalachian Mountain Club summer camp on Lake Winnepesaukee. I had a rudimentary idea of what I'd signed up for. I knew that the island, except for the main lodge, had no electricity, running water or flush toilets. Our cabins, sprinkled around the perimeter, were to be reached by a network of trails radiating out from the main lodge in the center of the island. I was prepared for the primitive nature of the experience; I'd always loved hiking and camping and having adventures in the wild. I didn't mind "roughing" it. However, I wasn't prepared for the aloneness of it. It is quite a different experience to venture out into the wilderness with your husband by your side than to face it alone. For the longest time we waited in the rain for the motorboat to take us across the lake to the island. At last, out of the darkness, the boat appeared. We piled in, and headed out across the bumpy waves. After finally docking at the island, we gathered up all our gear, located our cabin assignments and, with maps in hand, headed off into the dark night. From the dock, the large group of us wound our way up the trail to the main lodge. The rain dripping off my poncho and into my eyes made it hard to see, but I followed the bobbing lights ahead of me. We finally reached the central lodge and began descending from there to our various destinations on the other side of the island. Soon, the main trail fanned out, branching into many smaller trails, and my friends began splitting off to their individual cabins.

After I'd taken a right at the last fork, I discovered I was walking all alone on the trail. I had no idea how far I had to go – was it just around the next bend or another mile? I didn't know what would greet me when I found my cabin. I began to get cold; the rain came down harder, and my packs were getting heavier. My tears mixed with the raindrops streaming down my face. I wanted to succumb to my weariness, drop my duffle bags, let the pack slide from my back and collapse on a big boulder by the side of the path. I wanted to have a good cry. But I had to hold it together. So I got mad.

Where in the fuck are you, Ted? Why did you have to leave me?

This would have been an adventure with him - I could imagine the two of us laughing and joking as we slipped along the wet path, wondering what was in store for us. But without him, it was an interminable ordeal. As I picked my way along the rocky path, Ted's words kept echoing in my head:

"Just keep putting one foot in front of the other."

It became my mantra.

And then, a dream I'd had recently popped into my head.

I was on some hiking trip with Ted, and came across an old man making his way down a rocky trail. He was quite frail and his walking was precarious. As the old man was about to descend a steep slippery part of the trail, I called out for Ted to come and help. Then I realized Ted wasn't going to come, or come soon enough, and so I decided I'd better help the old man myself. The message was clear:

"You've got to help yourself. You're on your own, baby."

Ted may be in my heart giving me courage, but it's up to me as to where I place my foot.

Back to me walking on the trail: I was beginning to feel a little panicky, thinking I would never find my cabin. I wondered if I was still on the right path. And then suddenly, right before me, a dark square shape stood out against the nighttime sky. I had arrived. But the challenges were not over.

The dark shape turned out to be a 10-foot-square wooden cabin with a porch facing out toward the lake only a few feet away. It was dark. No lights anywhere; no stars, no moon. No other cabins were lit up. My mood was equally dark. I noticed that all the windows were boarded up.

I climbed up the three steps of the porch and tried the door, relieved to find it unlocked. I pushed the creaky door open and a musty smell hit me in the face. Apprehensively, I stepped inside and dumped my packs and sleeping bag on the two cot-like beds. Being alone in the cabin, I could spread out. (There! I'd found one advantage to being a widow!) A plastic washbasin and pitcher on one small wooden table and a kerosene lamp with a pack of matches on the other table were the only accoutrements of my new abode.

It seemed apparent that my next move was to light the kerosene lantern. I remembered my grandmother lighting a kerosene lamp like this at the ranch – fifty years ago. As a little girl, I'd never paid any attention to how she did it. I wondered if

I could blow up the cabin if I lit it the wrong way! Then, I discovered a small knob that rolled the wick up or down, and I gingerly put a match to the wick. Suddenly the inside of the cabin illuminated. Before I could celebrate my victory, a smoke alarm started screeching. What had I done wrong? What should I do?

About this time, I heard a friendly male voice outside the cabin calling out.

"Cindy, do you need some help?" I thought that might be a little obvious, but I was grateful.

My friend's husband came in.

"We need to get some air in here." He helped me pull up the heavy wooden shutters all around the cabin, secure the ropes on the hooks, and relight the lamp.

"I guess you're all set now," he said, and left.

"Thanks, I'm all set now," I responded to myself, trying to keep the sarcasm out of my voice. I unpacked some of my belongings, rolled out my sleeping bag and settled down for the night. Finally I could relax. *So here I am, by myself,* I thought with sadness and self-pity. *My new life.* But I was proud of myself, too... proud that I had gotten here, and found my spot.

I listened to the water gently lapping outside my door. As I heard the loons calling to each other across the lake, saying whatever loons say in the dark of the night, I imagined Ted out there somewhere, holding my hand in the dark.

Time Heals?

*"Grief comes to you all at once. So you think it will be over at once.
But it is your guest for a lifetime."*
Unknown

"Time heals," many people say. Or, *"Just give it time."*

While it's true that the passage of time blunts the sharp edges of pain, time, by itself, is neutral. The passage of time does take away the immediacy of sorrow, and gradually the pain becomes less acute. But it's what you *do* with time that makes the difference in how well you come through a significant loss.

The bereavement counselor who helped me the most during this time, Webb Brown, often said, "The best way to get to the other side of grief is not around it, or over it, or under it, but *through* the painful feelings."

Attempting to avoid the horrible feelings, which sometimes is essential for survival in the early days, ultimately serves only to delay the grieving process.

Yet when faced with crushing pain, the natural reaction is to want to avoid it. Seems like a no-brainer, right? We want to run away from pain or put up a wall to protect ourselves from feeling its full impact.

When our spouse dies, some of us might hole up in our house and make it a hiding place. Others, like myself, might make busyness a hiding place. I tried to escape the awfulness of going home to the empty house by creating a frenetic schedule of activities and keeping constantly on the go. I accepted nearly every invitation that came my way and was out almost every evening.

Stoicism is another way we attempt to build our armor and not feel the pain of our loss. Many of us have been socialized to not show our tears and sadness. We've been raised to believe that such feelings of vulnerability are a sign of weakness.

Buddhism teaches that what causes the real suffering is our very effort to *avoid* the pain. Resistance creates a knot of tension around the pain that actually amplifies the suffering.

I noticed an example of how this works one bitterly cold morning last winter as I walked to work. A ferocious wind was blowing and I felt chilled to the bone. I realized that my body was tense as a board. I had contracted every muscle in my shoulders and arms and chest in order to fend off the onslaught of frigid air. Becoming aware of how tense I was, I decided to try an experiment and consciously relax into the wind and let go of the tension in my muscles. To my amazement, most of my discomfort immediately lifted. I realized that I had been creating most of my suffering on my own by resisting the cold.

Similarly, if you were to tightly clench an ice cube in your fist, the cold would be unbearable. The tighter you squeeze, the more intense the cold is. But, if you open your fingers and allow the ice to gently rest in the open palm of your hand, the coldness of the ice would become quite bearable.

Grief that is avoided doesn't go away. Over time, the internalized grief takes its toll. Resistance calcifies the heart.

I was determined to use every resource I had to tackle my grief head on. I joined bereavement groups, met with my minister on a regular basis, resumed psychotherapy again, and attended workshops on grief and loss. And I talked to my friends. My friends made all the difference. They were my lifeline to the world of the living. Many of them had faced difficult life challenges of their own, and they had a large capacity to listen. They provided welcome respites in the storm and were generous with their presence and their time. I soon learned to avoid spending time with people with whom I'd have to put on a happy face and "make nice." I needed to be with people with whom I could be myself and share what I was going through.

I also read. Ever since I was a child, I have turned to books – for pleasure, for comfort and for learning how to face life's challenges. So it was not surprising that I turned to books for solace in my grief. I haunted the bookstores looking for the magic words that would take some of my pain away. I found the stories of other widows especially helpful as they echoed the depths of my own pain. I was not interested in reading a clinical analysis of grief. I needed to hear the stories of others who had been dropped into this desolate land and somehow had gotten through it and had gone on to make happy lives for themselves again. How did they do it? It was a mystery to me.

While I do believe that facing grief and feeling the full impact of the loss is important, I was surprised to discover that healing takes longer than I'd thought. A lot longer. When Ted died, in the back of my mind I had the idea that if I could face my grief directly and feel its full impact, then somehow I'd emerge, rather quickly, on the other side, relatively unscathed and ready to resume life again.

I remember walking into my first grief group, which happened to be an ongoing group, not the more typical short-term 6-8 session Bereavement Group. As members spoke, I learned that their spouses had been gone for a year or two or more – yet they were *still* coming to this group! I was repelled. No way did I intend to be still grieving two years from now. I didn't go back.

Little did I realize what was to come. This was not going to be a quick fix. It was not like there was a finite supply of tears inside me and once they were shed, I'd be done. My experience was about to teach me that it takes longer to get to the other side of grief than I'd ever imagined.

Widow's Group and Tales of Black Humor

"Bereavement is a darkness impenetrable to the imagination of the unbereaved."
Iris Murdoch
The Sacred and Profane Love Machine

After I'd had my initial foray into the bereavement group world and found that I was put off by people needing to attend meetings for a year or two after the death of their spouses, I came to my own realization. I didn't want to be without support entirely, and so believed if I could find a 6-8 week short-term bereavement group, I would be on my way to being healed. I've always known how helpful it is to talk to others who are going through what I am. I joined a series of short-term hospice bereavement groups. In time, a friend and I created what we call the *Good Grief Group* with some other widowed friends. We still get together to this day.

Nowhere do I feel more understood. We never hear those trite platitudes that attempt to slap a Band-Aid on a bleeding heart. Never expressed are veiled expectations that we should, "Be over it by now." Like survivors of a shipwreck who've been thrown together on an unfamiliar shore, we find safety and comfort in one another. As we recognize our sadness and pain in each other, we also see mirrored our own courage and resilience.

When a fellow grieving widow says that she knows what you mean by hating Saturday nights, or hating coming home to the empty house, or feeling enraged when the garbage disposal becomes jammed and there's no husband to fix it, I know she knows what I know. Together we laugh, we cry and we speak with an honesty that comes from having lost what mattered most. We have little use for facades or making nice. We share stories of heartache and envy when we see happy couples kissing on New Year's Eve, or planning their retirement or their next vacation together.

We try to remind ourselves of the wise words of Stephanie Ericsson:

"To envy another's situation is only a way that we compare our insides to another's outsides."

Many of these apparently happy couples may have troubles of their own that are not obvious to us.

We in the *Good Grief Group* heal each other with our dark humor. One of the widows told our group an amusing story about a recent visit to her doctor. After completing his examination, the doctor picked up the pen that she'd been writing with earlier and walked out of the examining room with it to make his clinical notes. A few moments later he came back in with a surprised and inquiring look on his face.

"This is *quite* an interesting pen you have here!"

She suddenly realized that the pen she, and then he, had been using was the vibrator pen she'd purchased some time earlier. Hiding her chagrin and without skipping a beat she nonchalantly replied.

"Yes, that's my widow's helper."

We laughed as we imagined that he probably had as good a tale to tell to his doctor cronies as she did sharing this with her widow buddies.

Other stories of black humor revolve around those irritating marketing calls. I shared with my group that sometimes when the voice on the phone asks to speak to Dr. Theodore Anderson, I say bluntly, "I'm sorry, he's dead" – which stops them dead in their tracks, a guaranteed way to bring a quick end to the conversation.

Another widow took a perverse pleasure in saying to telephone callers: "I'm sorry, he doesn't live here anymore." In answer to where her husband could be found, she replied, "In the ground at Pine Knoll Cemetery." When the same persistent caller telephoned again and asked to speak to her husband, she replied, "He's still dead."

We enjoyed coming up with new combinations of responses.

The day after Ted died, I received a call from the long-term care insurance company where we'd recently applied for coverage.

"Congratulations, we have good news for you, Mrs. Anderson. Your husband has been accepted for long term care insurance."

I spoke dryly in return.

"I have bad news for you, my husband died yesterday."

I told the group about how my daughter affectionately squeezed my shoulders as she walked by me at the table. It brought tears to my eyes. I realized how much I missed being touched. I lost many things when I lost my husband, but one of the hardest was never being touched. I shouldn't say "never" – I hugged my friends when we greeted each other, and once a month my beautician washed my hair. Other than that, days would go by when I would not be touched by another human being. Of course, I could always have paid someone for a massage, but it was the affection I was missing. I dearly loved those occasional visits when my grandchildren crawled up into my lap. It was the tenderness I loved, the warmth of skin on skin, the weight of feeling their little bodies nestled in my arms.

One day as my five-year-old grandson snuggled on my lap, I jokingly said to him, "Will you still let me hold you on my lap when you're grown up and big?"

"No, Grammy," Ian said. "I'm afraid I might break you."

We laughed as we discussed how widows are probably the only people who look forward to going through the security lines at the airport, hoping to get pulled aside for a "pat-down." One widow said, "I close my eyes and just enjoy the novelty of being touched."

Another asked when she'd been pulled aside at security, "Could I request having a man do my pat-down?" Someone else added: "Would you do it a little longer, sir? Ah yes, that's good. Do you have to stop now?"

We widows are grateful for small favors. One recommendation: British Airlines at Heathrow in London does the best pat-downs.

Over time, a bond of trust has developed between the members of our Good Grief Group that has made it possible to share with each other at greater levels of openness and honesty. We've revealed some of the not-so-good sides of our marriages. Some have talked about feeling relieved to be free of the long months, even years, of dealing with suffering and debilitating illness. Many of us have talked about really enjoying our new independence – like being able to have cereal for dinner if we don't feel like cooking.

We heal each other with our honesty, our shared tears, our scathing humor and our newfound strength.

We realize we don't have to die with the dead.

Ten Things Not To Say To A Widow
(And A Few Things You Should)

One day, my eight-year-old granddaughter asked me a question.

"Grammy, when are you going to kick the bucket?"

"I don't expect to die for a long time. And, oh by the way, most people use the word *die* rather than 'kick the bucket.'"

I found it refreshing to have her speak so naturally about this, a subject that many grown-ups feel awkward about and approach so tentatively. Young children have not yet learned that death is a loaded subject that should be handled delicately.

Yet when confronted with someone who has recently suffered a loss, people feel they need to say *something*. They may ask me, "How are you?" What a hard question. Do they really want to know, or are they just asking to be polite?

I know it's difficult for my friends and acquaintances to know what to say. Friends are torn between feeling genuine sympathy for me and also great relief for themselves. On some level, maybe not even a conscious one, a part of them is feeling, *Thank God this happened to you and not me. I'm glad it was your husband who died, not mine.* My suffering is like a preview of ghosts to come.

I don't know how open to be when someone asks me the question: "How are you?" Even if I were to try to answer honestly, it's often difficult. The fact is: I'm a moving target.

If we're talking about *right now*, this very moment, I'd say, "I'm fine." This morning, I was a puddle of tears – and last night, I was a raving idiot. Often I feel just neutral, normal (whatever that is). Sometimes, I actually feel happy! And then there are those times when I am so lonely from missing Ted that I feel my heart will break. *But, I don't know if you really want to hear all that.*

Nor is it helpful when someone says, "Let me know if there's anything I can do." In the early days of grief, I would not have been able to pick up the phone and ask for anything. I needed someone to *call me* and suggest getting together for a cup of tea. Or offer to go for a walk. Or drop over with a home-cooked meal for the two of us – not a meal for me to eat *alone.*

Asking for help has never been my strong suit, but I was better at accepting help when it was offered. One time, I came home after a long day's work thinking, *I should mow the lawn tonight.* As I drove into the driveway I said to myself, *It doesn't look so long.* And then I realized someone had cut it! My next-door neighbor had mowed my entire lawn. A gift from an angel. And this angel didn't mow my lawn just once.

I was fortunate that, for the most part, my friends and family were reasonably sensitive to what I was going through. Even though very few of my women friends were yet widowed, many of them had gone through heart-wrenching difficulties in their own lives. They were not afraid of painful feelings.

In spite of this, one comment I frequently heard that made me want to scream was, "At least he died doing what he loved." I tried to restrain myself from angrily retorting, "Rowing was just *one small part* of Ted's life that he loved. He loved many, many things, including his life with *me*!"

Most of the time, I was successful in just smiling and letting their comment pass. I know they meant to be helpful, but you can't sugar-coat death. It sucks. There's no other way to look at it. That's just the way it is.

In our widow's group, we've collected and shared the most memorable of the unhelpful, placating words we've received from well-intentioned people:

- "Just give it time. Time heals all wounds."
- "Be strong. Your children need you to be there for them."
- "You're young. You'll meet someone else."
- "Be thankful you had him as long as you did."
- "He's in a better place now."
- "At least you're keeping busy."
- "It was his time to go – he did what he came here to do."
- "At least you were together 35 years. I was with mine only 25."

Some people, uncomfortable with coming face-to-face with a grieving widow, avoid the subject of grief altogether. They go down a different aisle at the supermarket. They don't call or reach out, thinking, *She must need her space.* They may change the subject or avoid bringing up my husband's name for fear it'll make me sad or cry. The reality is that – I *am* sad. I'm always sad on the inside. Feeling tears coming to the surface is not a bad thing. It feels good to be real in the presence of a caring friend.

And finally, there are those hurtful words that convey an expectation that we *should be over it by now*. We should be moving on with our lives; we should begin thinking more about others, our children. My response to that: *grief knows no timetable*. Whether it is one year or many, grief cannot be hurried. These comments usually come from people who have not yet suffered the loss of someone precious to them. Our suffering makes them uncomfortable. Perhaps it's because they can't stand to see what they will be facing one day.

I know it's hard to be on the other end of the "death" conversation. The reality is that we all feel powerless in the face of death. What can a person say to us that will be empathic and show genuine caring? Our friends want to say something other than commenting on the weather, but *what*, exactly?

Welcome questions or opening comments might be:

- "How are you – I mean, how are you – <u>really</u>?"
- "I was thinking about you and wondering how your weekend went."
- "Are you sleeping?" ("Eating?"... "Getting out?")
- "How are your children doing? Do you see them much? "
- "I was thinking about you on this first (Easter-Passover-Thanksgiving-Christmas-Anniversary-Summer-Winter) without your husband. How is it for you? Do you have plans?"
- "I'm always just a phone call away. I'm usually up early or stay up late."
- Give a hug instead of saying something.
- Instead of "Call me if you need anything," offer something tangible that you can do and will do:
- "I can help you with thank-you notes."
- "I can pick up some groceries when I go to the store."
- "I'm always up for lunch, coffee, going for a walk, a movie."

And this I found especially helpful: *Speak the dead person's name.* Share your positive feelings about him/her; recall a favorite memory. We don't want them forgotten.

Sometimes people feel the need to cheer us up, or say something that will make us feel better. But most widows don't want to be *fixed*; they just want to be **heard**. We need the presence of a friend who cares.

Letting Go Of His Things

"It's not so bad that he died, it's that he stays dead."

Dianne Dahlbom

Some widows immediately want to empty the drawers and clear their husband's clothing out of the closets; keeping his clothing around is just too painful.

I felt the opposite. I wanted to hold onto Ted's things because they were all that remained of him. When I buried my head in his shirts and suits hanging forlornly on their hangers, I could almost smell his essence still lingering there.

But as time went by, I began to *want* more space. I decided it was time to take over Ted's half of the closet, instead of having to carry all my winter clothing upstairs in the spring and bring all my summer clothing down, and then a few months later reverse the process. It didn't seem he was coming back any time soon.

As I began sorting through Ted's nightstand drawer, his closet, his desk and files, I became aware that I wanted to find something meant for me from him. Maybe because I never got to say goodbye to him, I hoped I might find a last little gift. Perhaps he'd tucked away on a back closet shelf a little surprise for my 60th birthday party that we'd just planned to celebrate with the family. (Our surprise trip to Block Island was a special one just between the two of us.)

On Ted's first birthday after he died, I had a new idea. I invited my family over for a birthday dinner in his honor. When my grandchildren arrived, I spoke to them.

"Usually we bring a gift for the person whose birthday it is, but this year, the birthday boy isn't here. So we're going to do it the other way around. Granddaddy would want each of you to have a present from him. I know he would like you to look around the house, snoop in his drawers, explore his workshop, and pick out something special of his that you would like to keep."

The children had such fun roaming all over the house in search of a treasure, a remnant of the special man they called Granddaddy. After they'd each found something for themselves, I asked them to look around again and find something special that had belonged to granddaddy that they thought their cousins who lived in Colorado would like to have.

Later at the dinner table, we talked about what they had chosen and why it was meaningful. Five-year-old Dara had selected a shiny paperweight model of the earth. She remembered how precious the planet earth was to her granddaddy. He spoke with passion and urgency whenever he reminded us of our need to take care of it.

Her eight-year-old brother, Timmy, was a little boy fascinated by frogs, snakes and creatures of the outdoors. He was immediately drawn to the little orange and green beanbag frog that had perched itself on the couch in Ted's psychotherapy office. When I commented, "You and Granddaddy both love frogs," his response confirmed, "Yes, I'm a lot like Granddaddy." Tim, like many little boys, was also fascinated by long, pointy things, and would've selected the Maasai sword if we had let him. So instead, he chose the Maasai shield Ted had brought back from Kenya.

Eleven-year-old Alex had found a giant Mexican hat that reminded him of Granddaddy's goofy, fun-loving side. I know Ted would've been pleased knowing his grandchildren were taking home something tangible that would always remind them of him. We had fun that day—and I ended up feeling lighter, less weighed down by the past, and buoyed by the sense that I had disseminated something of Ted into the world.

There was another occasion near Christmas when what had started out as a fun day ended in tears. Brett and his family had come over to help me prepare for Christmas. We had bought a tree together, decorated it, made holiday cookies with the grandkids and enjoyed a delicious home-cooked dinner.

Later, I'd asked Brett if he'd like to take a look in dad's closet and see which of his father's things he might want. Brett set to work, stoically and methodically going through Ted's closet and bureau. He picked out a few ties, a jacket and some winter camping items. Suddenly he was undone. He broke down in tears.

"I don't want all this stuff! I want my dad!"

He sobbed and sobbed. Barbara and I put our arms around Brett and we all just stood there and cried, holding each other.

That night I dreamed that I was trying to catch a ball. If I caught the ball in just the right way, I'd be rewarded; I would be allowed to run with the ball up a long, winding ramp. I did this over and over. It was important to catch it correctly so that I could then run up the ramp. In the dream, I was surprised that I never seemed to get tired. No matter how many times I ran up the ramp, I never seemed to wear out. Running up the ramp was the exhilarating part.

In the morning, I wondered what the dream might have had to do with the events of the night before. Then, I had a realization: *Ted had given me that surprise gift I'd been looking for after all*. Not the tangible love letter I was looking for, or a present I could unwrap, but a message from beyond, the intangible. Perhaps Ted was communicating with me from another plane, and he was telling me that if I just hang in there and keep doing the work of grieving in the best way I know, it will take me to a better place. I will transcend this pain and sorrow. I have what it takes to do this.

I was struck by the similarity of my dream to the myth of Sisyphus who, as a punishment for his trickery and evil actions, was made to roll a huge boulder up a steep hill. Before it would reach the top, however, the massive stone would always roll back down, forcing him to begin again.

The difference between my dream and the myth was that, in my case, running up the hill was effortless – the reward for doing the hard work of grieving well. For Sisyphus, it was a maddening punishment. He was consigned to an eternity of useless effort and frustration, whereas I was promised that I would arrive at a place of freedom and happiness.

This Isn't My Job Description

"It's not about life getting easier, it's about you getting stronger."
Unknown

"Mom, you've got a situation in this drawer."

Brett's words drew my attention to a problem in my towel drawer that I hadn't wanted to acknowledge. For some time, I had been aware of some little black "crumbs" scattered in among the dishtowels – but I chose not to give them much thought.

Now I was forced to face the fact that I had mice residing in the soft folds of my dishtowels. The idea of these little creatures scampering through and snuggling among my towels at night gave me the creeps. *Ted, where in the hell are you anyway? I need my hunter here to deal with this.*

But no one else is living here now. So, I went to the hardware store and examined their assortment of poisons and traps that deal with rodents. I realized that I didn't have the heart, or stomach, to even use a "Have a Heart" trap. I didn't want to deal with a pathetic little living creature trapped in a cage peering out at me.

I finally settled on a mousetrap that seemed simple enough to operate – like opening a clothespin. I loaded it with peanut butter and gingerly placed it on top of the pile of dishtowels, closed the drawer and went away.

The next morning, I slowly pulled open the drawer with fear and trepidation. I was shocked and horrified to find a little gray mouse squashed beneath the wire jaws of my trap. I was both pleased with myself and appalled that I had put an end to the little creature's life on earth. I squeamishly lifted the trap out of the drawer and carried him (or her) to the far reaches of my yard and dropped it into the bushes. I wondered what little souls I had orphaned or widowed that day.

Over the next few days, I repeated this process again and again. Overall, I must have killed 6 or 8 little creatures – possibly a whole family of mice and their relatives. Now, every time I open the towel drawer, I am half expecting to see more little black crumbs, which means I'll have to go on a killing spree again. Maybe I'll have a heart the next time around.

Every time I lugged the trash out to the curb in the pouring rain or freezing snow, I was reminded of Ted – or rather the *absence* of Ted. Every household crisis that I faced: when the furnace quit working and the pipes froze; when the dripping faucet became a steady stream; when the AC broke and flooded the carpet; when the house became an eyesore and screamed to be painted. All this reminded me that Ted was no longer around to help out.

Sometimes, I got angry towards him. *You don't have to mow the lawn, or shovel the driveway or pay the bills or worry if you have enough money to retire. You got off easy, Ted! You left me holding the bag!*

70

When I was faced with having to deal with things falling apart or some mechanical emergency, I felt not only anxious, but also angry. In addition to the challenge of handling the situation, I felt mad that *I* had to do it.

"Ted," I'd said aloud, "This is supposed to be your job! You were the hunter, the warrior, the protector of our home. This is outside my job description."

What was the universe's answer?

"Well honey, welcome to your new life. Get used to it. Maybe it wasn't something you were responsible for when you were married, but your job description has changed. You are a widow. Now, you handle everything!"

Having to deal with these crises that had been Ted's domain only emphasized my aloneness. At a time when necessity required that I be stronger and more competent, I felt more fragile and weak. But, there was an unexpected upside to all this. Rather than allowing myself to disintegrate into tears of helplessness, my anger helped keep me strong.

Going back to the mice situation, once I had successfully captured the first little mouse and carried it out and dumped it in the woods, I released it from the trap with the exclamation, "There, you fucker!" These words were addressed not to the poor little dead mouse, but to Ted, whom I imagined was watching me from somewhere. On another occasion, a similar epitaph followed when I figured out how to replace my cracked toilet seat with a brand new one. "There, you fucker, I did it!"

One day, I was returning home from western Massachusetts by myself. On this long drive home, my car suddenly went haywire. The needles on my dashboard started swinging wildly and the car started running erratically. Something was terribly wrong. I was both panicked and angry. My new mantra, *Where in the hell are you, Ted?* was on my lips again. Cars that break down; roofs that begin leaking; TVs that go on the fritz; computers that get infected; taxes that have to get figured; fluorescent light bulbs that need replacing – these are all a normal part of life. But for the widow who's used to sharing the running of the household, it's a doubly hard challenge. We have to do it *all* by ourselves, now.

Ted and I had a very workable division of labor. We each had certain strengths and areas of expertise. Ted was mechanically gifted; he enjoyed fixing things. He also was steady and calm in the face of life's crises. In the past when I had panicked over a car that was misbehaving or a bat that was flying inside our cottage, he calmly handled the situation.

I, of course, had my own areas of competence. I was the chief cook, cleaner and bottle washer – and the social director. If I had been the one to die first, Ted would have been up a creek trying to remember our four children's and eight grandchildren's birthdays, and how to manage future Christmases.

One of the amazing transformations on my journey through grief was my increasing competence in handling these day-to-day challenges. On one of my out-of-town trips, I got a rental car, and as I went about figuring out the strange arrangement of switches and buttons on the temporary vehicle, I noticed that my anger was gone. Absent was my frustrated, *Where the fuck are you Ted?!*

In its place was simply a pride in having mastering this latest challenge.

Life Changes In A Flash

As a widow, you wouldn't think I would have needed any more lessons in the fragility and unpredictability of life. Ted's death should have given me my full quota of this brutal lesson for one lifetime. But that's the whole point: we have no control over fate other than in retrospect, when we think about what we should have/could have done.

Often in the summers, I've gone out to Colorado for a vacation in the heart of the Rockies. After Ted died, I had purchased a little condo with Scott and Debbie not far from where I grew up on my grandparents' ranch. It became a fun way to spend time with them and my two grandsons, Nathan and Kenny.

One day, the five of us decided to go on a bicycle ride around the lake. I got ready quickly and waited while Scott busied himself getting the boys' bikes ready and Debbie gathered last minute snacks and rain gear for the kids. To pass the time, I decided to adjust the strap on my helmet, which had always sat on my head in a rather cock-eyed fashion, slipping to one side or the other when I leaned over the handlebars to pedal. Finally we were ready to go.

I was thrilled to be taking this ride with Scott and his family, but I didn't want to be a drag. Scott is a serious cyclist and competes in many challenging bicycle events. He is raising his sons to follow in his bicycle tracks. Twelve-year-old Nathan is on a team and races every weekend.

As we pedaled along the paved bike path, I felt relieved that I was holding my own. Of course, it helped that I was riding a bicycle with skinny tires and the rest of them rode mountain bikes with fat, knobby wheels.

After a while I began feeling a little cocky and thought, *I'm going to have a little fun with these boys.* So I picked up my speed, pulled alongside Nathan and announced provocatively:

"On your left!"

I zoomed past Nathan down the path. Now, I was in the front of the pack with Nathan behind me and Kenny, Scott and Debbie bringing up the rear. We were flying. Suddenly, I saw that the path ahead of me was making a sharp turn to the right. At almost the same instant, I saw two riders approaching me from the other direction. I was still in the left lane of the bike path and I knew I had to slow down and get over to the right lane immediately or we'd have a head-on collision.

I put on my brakes and quickly turned my handlebars to the right. A recipe for disaster! My bike skidded out from underneath me and I landed on my right side, hitting my head on the hard pavement. It all happened in a flash. Almost immediately, I heard a cyclist shout, "She hit her head, she hit her head!" as Scott and Debbie pedaled up.

One look at my cracked helmet confirmed that indeed, I had hit my head. I lay splattered in the middle of the bike path in a daze. The entire right side of my body felt on fire. I also felt mortified. Here I was causing all this commotion, and I had so much not wanted to be a drag on my family.

I heard someone say that I'd better get off the pavement or another biker would crash into me. I managed to scoot my body off to the side. As I lay there in the dirt, I spoke to Scott and Debbie.

"Why don't you go on with the kids and I'll rest awhile and then ride back to the condo."

I didn't even know if my bike still worked. My brain was obviously not fully functional. Fortunately, Scott and Debbie had better sense and were not about to go off and leave me in a heap on the side of the road.

Scott decided to pedal home, bring the car, and then Debbie would drive me to the emergency room while Scott and the boys continued their ride. I don't know how I managed to walk the twenty feet over to a picnic table where I waited for him to return.

As I sat there, the pain descended and I began to feel dizzy and nauseous. I put my head down on the table and waited. When Scott arrived with the car I tried to stand up to walk, but now the pain in my pelvis was unbearable. It was impossible to put any weight on my right leg.

After a long wait in the ER, I learned the outcome – I'd fractured my pelvis, fractured my elbow and split open my helmet. Thanks to that well-fitting helmet, I had not cracked my skull! It had saved me from becoming a huge nuisance to my children for years to come.

Months later, after progressing through crutches, a cane, a cast on my arm and two surgeries, I emerged with a healthy body. Looking back, I have many to whom I am grateful: to Debbie, who lovingly held my hand as I lay in pain in the ER; to Scott for tenderly washing my hair in the kitchen sink every morning; and to Nathan and Kenny, who often came into my makeshift bedroom in their dining room and sweetly asked, "How are you feeling, Grammy?" After I returned home to Lexington, I was grateful to my family and friends who brought meals, shopped for me and drove me to appointments.

I am also grateful for the Buddhist wisdom of impermanence I'd gained along the way. Everything changes. From the beginning of this accident, I was able to look at this whole experience as passing phenomena. All of the pain I was going through was temporary, and I knew it. When I'd hobble around with a cane, my hip aching and my arm in a sling; when I'd go to work with my hair a mess because I couldn't use my right arm to properly blow dry it; when the doctor took the cast off and announced the fracture had not healed – that, in fact, it had widened and would need surgery; when I slipped on the ice and my newly recovering elbow hit the edge of the porch steps exactly at the point of the surgery – throughout all of this I was able to maintain the perspective that this was all transitory. I knew I would heal. Which is not to say there were not nights when I'd awaken and my elbow would be throbbing so intensely that I'd be brought to tears. But, I was able to remove myself from the pain by saying to myself: *This injury has happened to my body – it has not happened to Me.* I am the observer, witnessing my body going through all this. I am not my body. I am not the pain, the fear nor the worry. These are all impermanent. They come and they will go.

And last, I am grateful for another unexpected benefit I gained along the way.

As I mentioned above, I fell on the icy steps at home shortly after the surgery to my arm. I developed a huge hematoma the size of a golf ball on my elbow near the fracture site. The doctor asked me to elevate my arm by sleeping with a pillow under it. Later on, after I'd healed, I'd still found something comforting about wrapping my arm around the pillow and holding it close to my body. Hugging the soft roundness had become strangely soothing when I crawled into the empty bed at night. I called it my transitional object. Like the young child who finds a security blanket to provide her psychological comfort when mother is not around, say at bedtime, I found the soft pillow a comforting presence.

I could almost imagine I was holding Ted in my arms.

Finding My Voice

"Take your best pony and ride into your fear."

Sioux Prayer

In his last years, Ted had frequently said these words:

"If anything ever happens to me, just call up Mr. Smith (not his real name) and he'll take good care of you."

Mr. Smith was our long-time attorney who had written our wills, drawn up the legal papers for Ted's professional corporation, and taken care of other legal needs over the years. Ted assured me I would be in good hands.

As instructed, when Ted died, I called up Mr. Smith. A few days after Ted's death, Karyn and I arrived at his office. We were ushered into a boardroom and seated at a long polished, mahogany conference table. There we sat, feeling alone and bewildered.

After what seemed like a long while, the attorney walked in briskly. He carried a sheaf of files and was followed by his paralegal. He marched over, and without looking us in our eyes, shook our hands and spoke rather formally.

"I'm sorry about your loss."

He didn't ask us anything about ourselves or share any of his thoughts or memories of Ted. Instead, he began detailing all the legal duties he would be performing. He told us that settling Ted's estate and filing the taxes was a simple, straightforward matter; there was nothing complicated involved. I listened to him continue for a while, and then asked my question.

"How much is this going to cost?"

When he hesitated, I continued.

"Just give us a ball park estimate."

He replied, "Around $10,000."

We left feeling stunned.

If he had shown a little kindness or compassion, I'm sure we would have proceeded without a question. But he had treated us so coldly that I was appalled.

I called a good friend and told her of our awful experience. Jennifer gave me the name of her attorney, whom she highly recommended.

A couple of days later, Karyn and I walked into this new attorney's office feeling apprehensive and nervous. He greeted us warmly and I immediately began to feel I was in good hands. He took the time to get to know us. He wanted to know what Ted was like as a person, how he had died and how we were doing. He cared. Only after we'd gotten to know each other did we get to the business of Ted's estate. When I asked him what he would charge, he responded.

"About $2,500."

My first independent act as a widow was to fire Ted's attorney. I called Mr. Smith's office, told him I would not be continuing with him, and that I would come over and pick up my files.

A few weeks later he sent me his bill for our brief appointment. An exorbitant figure! In addition to the fees for himself and his paralegal for our appointment, he padded the invoice with additional charges for "reviewing documents and insurance consultation." This latter item was totally irrelevant since Ted had *no* insurance!

I was furious. I felt he was taking advantage of me – a grieving widow who didn't know much about financial and legal matters. At least I did have access to my rage.

I took great pleasure in writing a letter to him explaining why I was only paying a portion of his bill – his fee for the hour's consultation. Furthermore, I wrote:

"In this post-9/11 era (the destruction of Manhattan's twin towers had occurred only a month after Ted's death), we hear countless reports of strangers reaching out in compassion, sometimes even sacrificing their lives to help someone in need."

I told him how my new accountant had come to my house, talked with us for over an hour about his fond memories of Ted before he ever began the conversation around our accounting business. What was his fee for the visit? "$ 0."

I said I didn't expect him not to charge me, but I had expected more warmth and compassion from someone who had known Ted as well as he had. He never responded to my letter.

Only later did I realize that I was also grateful to Mr. Smith for giving me the opportunity to vent my anger. Along with the outrage I felt toward this cold, money-driven attorney, I recognized that my anger had other sources. I was angry at Ted for having died on me, and for my whole situation of being a 60-year-old widow facing perhaps another 25 to 30 years of living without my dear husband.

Magical Thinking

"I'm tired of being the brave little widow."

Dianne Dahlbom

My widow friend sat with me in the audience of the First Parish's Annual Auction. One of us remarked to the other about how hot the room was. I said to friend, "I'd take off my sweater and sit here in my bra if it'd bring Ted back." I knew I could be silly with her, and before long we were both laughing and imagining ourselves, two older ladies sitting there in the audience very politely and seriously paying attention to the goings-on, but essentially naked from the waist up. We fantasized that if anyone commented on our bizarre behavior, we'd patiently explain to them that our husbands would be arriving soon. We had fun that night.

Most people are probably familiar with Elisabeth Kübler-Ross' ground-breaking delineation of the five stages of grief that a person goes through when faced with profound loss: denial, anger, bargaining, depression and acceptance. We don't proceed through these steps in an orderly procession; most often there is an overlap, and, in my case, bargaining was present throughout the other stages. Actually in recent years, an additional stage has been added to these five stages – and that is of meaning-reconstruction. In this contemporary approach to grief therapy, successful grieving is viewed as the bereaved person finding meaning or significance in the suffering. Thus, there does not need to be a withdrawal of psychic energy from those we have loved and lost, but rather we may continue to sustain a connection with our deceased loved one as we integrate this loss into our lives.

I was well aware of these stages through my work as a clinical social worker, and I could see how I had gone through denial and anger and certainly sadness and depression. But I was amused to see how *bargaining* showed up in my own grieving process. I've been surprised by some of the strange bargains my mind has conceived of in its unconscious attempt to magically bring Ted back. While my conscious self knew very well that my husband was dead and would never return, my unconscious self still had trouble accepting the finality of it.

For instance, my first, *I'd do anything if it would bring Ted back,* was, *I'd take off all my clothes and run through the streets of Lexington naked if it would bring Ted back.* Or, *I'd give a speech in front of 3,000 people if it'd bring Ted back,* or, *I'd live with Ted in a tent in the Sahara Desert for the rest of my life if...* or, I'd quit my job and dig ditches if... or *I'd jump out of an airplane (with a parachute) if I could have Ted back.*

These random thoughts often popped into my head, and not only when I was feeling particularly sad or missing Ted. Often they were kind of silly like, *I'd crawl to work on my hands and knees if...*

The various bargaining ideas my mind came up with seemed to involve doing some kind of behavior that was either embarrassing, arduous, frightening, challenging, or just plain ridiculous, like, *I'd cut this entire lawn with a pair of scissors...*

I never thought for a moment that if I did any of these things my husband would actually return. These random thoughts represented my feeling that I would do anything, short of harming myself or someone else, if it would bring my husband back to me.

Over time these bargaining thoughts gradually faded away. But even several years after my husband's death, these thoughts occasionally popped into my head. They showed me how close to the surface my longing for Ted still lived inside of me.

You Are What You Love

When it is the darkest, you can see the stars.
Ralph Waldo Emerson

It's about 2 o'clock in the morning, and I'm wide awake.

My head is filled with the bleakest of thoughts. Last night, I was out with several couples. They had all been a big part of our married life in the past. As the evening unfolded, I became increasingly aware of missing my husband. Ted's absence was almost like a presence itself, a lonely presence sitting there next to me at the table. I found the closeness of these other couples painful to witness. When one couple playfully reminisced about their vacation in Hawaii, or another talked excitedly about their plans to remodel their kitchen, or when one woman slipped her hand inside her husband's as they waved goodbye and walked down the sidewalk, it only made me long, all the more, for that easy familiarity Ted and I had once shared. If he had been with me that evening, we would have had our own fun stories to share. Many a knowing look would have passed between our eyes. Because I was feeling increasingly apart from others as the evening wore on, I found it hard to give voice to these thoughts, although I had no shortage of happy memories. I guess I was still too wounded.

Later that night, lying alone in the dark of my bed, my thoughts began to pull me down the slippery slope to a place of no good. I felt the lives of all those couples were moving along flawlessly while mine was derailed. A small (very small) part of me vicariously enjoyed their affection and easy comfort with each other, and yet most of me felt increasingly separate and adrift.

On one level, I knew it was just my thoughts creating this misery for myself. *My thoughts are not Me.* They are impermanent and temporary, and tomorrow life will probably look a whole lot better.

Even with this awareness, I wasn't yet able to stop my thoughts from doing their damage. They proliferated. Sometimes, I'd found the writings of various Buddhist teachers – Pema Chodron, Stephen Levine, Jack Kornfield – wonderfully helpful, and sometimes all their good words hadn't worked at all. Grief just plain hurt. Or, in the language of my children, "It sucks." Dark thoughts led to even darker thoughts. Life felt pointless. Writing this story seemed stupid, irrelevant. I tossed and I turned and I turned and I tossed. *Gotta get to sleep.* Sleep didn't come.

I'll try meditating, I said to myself. *I always doze off when I meditate,* I thought. I focused on my breathing, but my thoughts wouldn't stay put for more than four or five breaths. *This isn't working. I will just have to wait out the interminable night. The morning sunlight will wash away the darkness and cast a very different glow over my day.* But within myself, I had really wanted to find the resources, the wherewithal, not to allow those lonely thoughts to have such power over me.

That night, after meeting with the couples and having such a hard time recuperating, I decided to turn the light on and read something, anything, to get my mind in a different place. And suddenly a realization hit me as I was reading: *You are what you love, not what loves you. And no one can take that away.*

I realized that in any of the loving relationships that I have ever had, whether it was loving Ted, or my children, my grandchildren, even the affection I felt for my dog, what has given me the greatest happiness is the love *I have felt* and expressed toward the other. Being loved in return is a bonus, a karmic dividend. The true source of my happiness has always been in feeling tenderness and love arising *within myself,* and in reaching out to give expression to it.

The realization is that *it is the loving, not the being loved, that gives me the greatest joy.* This becomes clearer whenever I think of examples to the contrary.

Since Ted's death, I have dated several men (sequentially). A couple of men along the way had cared a lot about me, even said they loved me. But I could not feel that same love in my heart for them. Love, that mystery of mysteries, that indefinable spark, just didn't ignite. I could not feel, or show, the kind of tenderness that I knew I had within me. As a result, the relationships were ultimately unsatisfying.

With these experiences, I came to believe what I had initially thought with Ted's death: that romantic love was removed forever from my life. Ted would never again hold me in his arms. He would not kiss me or caress me, or show that he loved me. Yet, although it is true that Ted's death took the physical manifestation of *his* love for me away, I realized that our love for each other was still inside me and that it is something I will never lose. Through having loved Ted so deeply, my heart had been opened. My capacity for loving had been enlarged and expanded. Similarly, if I had lived in a hateful relationship for all those many years, the hating would have poisoned me. I would have been made smaller, more constricted. My heart would have shrunk. Ted shaped who I am today, just as I know I influenced him. *I am whom I have loved.*

Sometimes when I feel sorry for myself, all I have to do is realize that I've been overlooking the *capacity* to love that I carry within me. I have the power to make myself happy any old time. I simply have to open my eyes, look around me, and reach out with love to someone or something. I can bring joy to myself whenever I please. There's always someone who would appreciate a pat on the back, a word of encouragement, a call to let them know I'm thinking of them, someone who'd enjoy my celebrating with them a success they've had. Even smiling at a stranger can lift my spirits.

Along with the realization that came to me that night – that it is the loving, not the being loved, that really matters – the barest glimmer of a new thought began to edge itself into my consciousness. I thought, perhaps, just maybe, my capacity to feel that spark of love for another man might one day come into my life again. This new idea first came to me that night, but it would be many months before I would actually feel it showing up in my life.

Sometimes, when I am having trouble falling asleep at night, I find it helpful to rest in the memory of a loving time with Ted or my children or grandchildren. In this tranquil state, sleep can come upon me without my having to work so hard to make it happen.

Gift In The Wound

"Life will break you. Nobody can protect you from that, and living alone won't either. For solitude will also break you with its yearnings. You have to love. You have to feel. It is the reason you are here on earth. You are here to risk your heart. You are here to be swallowed up. And when it happens that you are broken, or betrayed, or left, or hurt, or death brushes near, let yourself sit by an apple tree and listen to the apples falling all around you in heaps, wasting their sweetness. Tell yourself that you tasted as many as you could."

Louise Erdrich
The Painted Drum

When Ted died, I had a hope in the back of my mind – one that I barely articulated even to myself. I hoped that not only would I survive Ted's death, but over time I would gain something for having gone through all of this. I did not want to end up diminished as a person from having lost my beloved husband. That would not be honoring Ted or what he would have wanted for me. Writings by wise teachers like Pema Chodron reinforced this desire:

"Let the sharpness of difficult times pierce the heart, let these times humble us and make us wiser and more brave. Let difficulty transform you. And it will. We just need not to run away."

Opening to the suffering is healing, not because the suffering itself is noble, but because of the *attitude of openness* one cultivates in facing it. When a friend reaches out and asks, "How are you doing?" I try to welcome her interest and respond authentically. This leads to a deepening of our friendship as we both develop greater closeness and empathy.

The amazing thing I have often experienced is that, after having weathered the storms of sadness, an unexpected gift has come my way; perhaps something like a dazzling rainbow; perhaps a period of calm and peace. Sometimes even glimmers of joy.

Over the days and months, and, yes, the years of missing Ted, the waves of grief have worked their healing magic. Now they come only rarely. The sadness has essentially cleared out and I'm left with all the rich and happy memories of Ted etched deeply in my heart.

Perhaps when faced with having lost someone dear to us, our heart has to expand in order to contain the sheer enormity of the sadness. It gets stretched and softened over time. Like the Grand Canyon, whose crevasses have deepened and enlarged over the centuries as the streams and rivers and the ravages of weather have washed through it, so we, too, are expanded as life runs through us. We move out of our small self-absorbed world and let our pain connect us to all of life. As our heart expands, we can experience the greater world. When you bear the unbearable, something is irrevocably changed. You emerge from the pain a different person.

My heart is like the balloon that has been blown up, almost to the point of breaking, over and over again. At first, my heart was stiff and difficult to open, but in time, it has become soft and pliable. It has now become so stretched that it easily expands to experience intense emotions, and not just the painful ones. I can be as deeply moved by something beautiful or joyful as something sad. The tears that well up feel more like an opening of my heart than a falling apart of my life. Tears filled my eyes one day when I saw my little five-year-old granddaughter tenderly stop her playing to help her little brother who had just fallen down and skinned his knee. Or when she lovingly put her arm around him after he peed in the toilet for the first time saying, "Good job, Buddy Boy!"

One evening, I went with some friends to the opera, *The Marriage of Figaro*. As the poignant, achingly beautiful voice of the soprano soared to the upper reaches of the balcony where I was sitting, my heart was in shreds. I emerged from the theater with tears still running down my cheeks. My tears that night were not the tears of sadness and loneliness, but tears of great joy for being able to re-connect with my own love for a man that had at times soared to such heights. It doesn't take much at all to pierce my heart. And for this I am most grateful.

Kissing Frogs

"A turning point
May have no words
But these occur
Will have to do.
As markers for the crucible
That moving forward must pass through

For only after grief is grieved
That tears the rugged soul apart
Is space re-made for love received
Into opening of heart."

Barbara Pizer

Several years before Ted died, when a good friend of mine became widowed, I felt sorry for her as she faced the prospects of dating again. *I'd hate to be in her shoes,* I thought.

And so here I am, walking in those same shoes. I imagine some of my married friends have similar thoughts about me when they hear the ups and downs of my dating efforts.

As I posted my profile for the first time on an internet dating site, I couldn't believe I had come to this: having to advertise myself to get a date! Ted used to say, "If I die, the men will be beating down your door." Yeah, right. My door seems to be faring pretty well, thank you.

First of all, except for men I deemed grossly inappropriate (too old, too fat, too short, too uneducated, too dorky), rarely did a man select me. I had to be the one to take the initiative and make the first contact. Not easy to do for a child of the fifties who is accustomed to the man being the aggressor. I would summon all my chutzpah and let a guy know I was interested in him. We'd e-mail back and forth a few times, talk on the phone, and then set up the big first date to meet in person.

I'd get all gussied up – buy a new outfit to look more contemporary, get my hair colored to look younger, buy a new bra to look less saggy, even put on some eye makeup for a change – and head out to the restaurant or coffee shop where we'd agreed to meet. Because I was usually anxious, I'd arrive ten to fifteen minutes early and sit in the car reviewing the notes I'd made about my prospective date from our previous e-mails and phone conversations. Hopefully, I'd be able to remember if he was the one who was twice divorced with three children and had traveled to Turkey, or the one with four grandchildren who'd been divorced only once and then widowed and who liked to sail? I usually waited to go in until a couple of minutes after we'd planned to meet. *Mustn't look too eager.*

As I drove to the different restaurants to meet these dates, I'd be envisioning the man of my dreams. I was as nervous as a schoolgirl and my hopes were out the roof. *Maybe this would be the one.* With great anticipation, I'd walk in through the door wondering who was going to be greeting me. I'd take one look at him, and my heart would sink. I felt like Goldilocks. *This one's too short! This one's too fat! This one's got too much hair on his face! This one's too cold and intellectual! This one's not intellectual enough!* Later, I'd say to myself, *For Heaven's sake! Stop being so critical! Give the guy a chance.*

We'd meet, we'd talk and then we'd part. And then would come the crash. I'd drive home feeling let down, defeated and discouraged. Most of the time, I had no interest in seeing the guy again. Once in a great while, when I did find someone attractive, he wasn't interested in me. I'd ask myself, *How is it that the most wonderful man in the world could have found me beautiful, sexy and lovable, and this jerk couldn't care less!*

One time, I had driven for over an hour to the agreed upon restaurant. Because I had gotten a little lost on my way, I had given my date a call to let him know I'd be arriving soon. I walked in, glanced around, and found that no one seemed to be waiting for me – just a man sitting off to the side engrossed in his book. Since I saw no one else, I walked up to him and asked if he was so-and-so. He looked up and said yes. I was surprised. *He hadn't even been watching out for me*, I thought. *Not a good start.* Dinner proceeded and he was still in his own world. He talked on and on about himself while I waited for him to ask me something about myself, but not a single question. Nothing. I thought, *Maybe he's nervous and feels he needs to impress me, or he thinks it would be intrusive to inquire about me.* So occasionally, I tried interrupting his monologue and inserting some information about myself. But did he pick up on this and realize there was someone else at the table? No. He simply used this as a stimulus to go back to himself. By the time the dinner arrived I was thinking, *Get me out of here!* Then, it was just a matter of getting through the rest of the meal as quickly as possible. I was no longer present. I just nodded my head, and went through the motions of listening. When the check came, I decided that, rather than offering to chip in on the bill as I usually do, I would just let him pick it up. It was all about him, anyway. As I drove home in the dark that night, the rain that poured down on the windshield matched the tears that poured down my cheeks.

The disappointment and letdown of experiences like that only re-opened my broken heart and intensified my longing for Ted. After one of these dating attempts, it always took me a while to recover. I wondered why I put myself through this exercise in self- torture.

The bottom line is that Ted was a hard act to follow. When I met him, I was swept off my feet on the first date. Now, I sometimes wonder if that was a once-in-my-lifetime happening. Being older now and not as naïve and unshaped by life as I had been then, I think *perhaps it'll take longer now*. So I tried to give each new date the benefit of the doubt, hoping that in time one of these guys would grow on me. I learned after a few of these encounters, however, not to go back for a second date. I had kissed a lot of frogs along the way, and sometimes I kissed them way too long, thinking they'd metamorphose. Too often, I hung in there longer than I should have. Rather than having my feelings deepen for this prospective love interest, an aversion would set in. What I've come to know about myself is that if I can't feel "in-love" with a man, if that certain indefinable spark or chemistry doesn't exist, the sexual passion can't happen either.

How do you know a good man when you find him? When I come home from a date feeling I've been invisible to the guy, and I feel myself receding and shutting down; when I feel my thoughts turn critical and fault-finding; when I feel all the aliveness within me shrivel up – then I know this is not a good potential relationship for me. I've learned that the most important question to ask myself is not how do I feel about this guy, but how do I feel about <u>myself</u> when I am with him? A good relationship brings out the best in both people. Do we both feel energized, appreciated, celebrated, happy, open and alive when we're with each other?

When I met Ted, I wasn't even looking for a man, and then he just walked into my life with no effort on my part. Maybe it will be like that again with someone else.

And, maybe not. No matter how many times I was willing to try to find the right new partner, I was also aware that I certainly didn't want the value of the rest of my life to be defined by the presence or absence of a man. I didn't want to believe that without a man in my life, I couldn't be happy. I wanted to feel grateful for what I had and have – and that is a lot – rather than be focused on what was missing.

So I had arrived at the point where I said to myself, *I'm going to bag it, hang it up. I'm not going to get out and beat the bushes again. I'm not going to climb on that old merry-go-round any more. If it happens, it will happen. I'm not going to close the door, but I'm not holding it open for the wrong guy, either.*

De-pedestalizing Ted

There was one interesting realization I gained from dating. Trying to understand all these other men let me see how much I idealized Ted. I had gone back into therapy for help with my grief, but now wanted help to look at my relationship with Ted more realistically. From the time I first met Ted, I had always looked up to him. He was ten years older than I was, a man (in an era when women had been raised to be subservient to men), and a psychiatrist (and I, a clinical social worker). Ted was already a father when I met him, whereas I was relatively inexperienced with children except for some camp counseling experience. Over the years, our relationship became more equalized as we faced life's challenges together. But at the deepest level, my early feelings towards Ted remained locked securely in place.

I realized that I needed to see Ted more realistically before I would ever be able to appreciate a new man in my life, and see him for who he might be. As long as I had my husband on a pedestal, no man stood a chance of entering my heart. There is room for only one man on top of a pedestal.

It's interesting how grief can shine a rosy glow over our dead loved ones. The lines in May Sarton's poem, "All Souls," say it well:

"...*Now the dead move through all of us still glowing...*
  ...And memory makes kings and queens of (them)..."

To read the poem in its entirety, see the future chapter titled, "You Don't Ever Have To Let Go."

Idealizing our dead mates is one way we may unwittingly protect ourselves from having our hearts broken again. Anyone we come to care about is going to abandon us one day (unless we are the one to go first the next time).

It's not that I thought Ted didn't have his faults or that we didn't have our problems as a couple; quite the contrary. The thing that made the difference for our marriage is that we could talk about what was upsetting us. Sometimes we'd get very angry at each other for one thing or another and we'd go round and around. Occasionally, while we were in the middle of a heated argument, I'd think to myself, *I don't see how we can survive this argument. This may be our undoing.* But we'd hang in there, talking and trying to listen, until we'd come through it to the other side, both of us with a better understanding of where the other was coming from. And we'd each have a plan for how we, ourselves, could handle this issue in the future. Not that we were always successful with this, but the important thing was how much closer we always felt after one of these encounters.

Sometimes I'd get aggravated with Ted for dominating a dinner party conversation with what I thought others would think were his outlandish ideas. For example, Ted dearly loved the natural world and was passionate about our need to take care of our precious earth. He would become aggravated with how people and nations live with a flat-earth mentality. "If you don't like something, you can just send it out of town – your garbage, your nuclear waste, anything unwanted." He wanted to change society's attitudes by changing people's language in order to reflect a round-earth reality. Instead of saying the sun "rises" and the sun "sets," he wanted to teach people to say the earth "rolls toward" and "rolls away" from the sun. When he'd go on and on with these things at a social gathering, I'd feel embarrassed and apologetic for him.

On the way home, I'd say, "Honey, you were not having a dialogue with people. You were not listening to what they had to say."

And he'd respond by saying, "I know I talked a lot, but I'm lonely. I'm just trying to get their attention."

This, of course, made my heart melt. His openness about his insecurity only made me love him all the more. Back on the pedestal he'd go.

Just as Ted couldn't move over to let someone else into the conversation, now I was having trouble moving him over in my heart in order to let someone else into my life.

It is a tall order to come to love someone *else* later in life. When I met Ted, he had been a handsome, athletically built young man with an appealing, boyish charm. Even as his body aged and he'd lost some of that youthful charisma, I saw beyond the wrinkles and thinning hair. I still remembered him as that 35 year-old-man who'd walked into my life so many years earlier. Now, in meeting someone new, I wouldn't have the opportunity to have that longitudinal view. Likewise, I realized that a new man would see me as a 70-year-old woman with all her signs of aging, not as that pretty young woman who had captured Ted's heart so long ago.

One of the ideas that helped me to stop comparing a new man to Ted was to stop viewing this new person through the old lens of, *Is he better or worse than my husband?* – and instead, see him as *different*. He has a *different body build, different profession, different mannerisms, different life experiences,* and so on. This was not a competition. This manner of thinking allows me to have Ted remain special in all *his* ways, and a new man to become special in *different* ways.

So life goes on. It's a work in progress.

Willingness to Hazard Ourselves

"...When it's over, I want to say: all my life
I was a bride married to amazement.
I was the bridegroom, taking the world into my arms.
When it's over I don't want to wonder
if I have made of my life something particular, and real.
I don't want to find myself sighing and frightened,
or full of argument.
I don't want to end up simply having visited this world."

Mary Oliver
"When Death Comes"

One day when I was babysitting my 4 and 6 year-old grandchildren, I decided to take them to the town pool where I have fond memories of bringing my own children some thirty years ago. I was hoping to share with them the joy and exuberance I remember so vividly. The water was chilly, and this was the first time Skyler and Ian had been here. They were tentative and reluctant to get involved. And so was I. I sat on the edge, or walked around the baby pool encouraging them to get wet. And yet, the truth of the matter was that *I didn't want to get my hair wet!* The thought came to me, *We could be having a lot more fun than we're having.* So I said to myself, *For heaven's sake, to hell with your hair!*

I called out to my grandkids.

"Hey, let's go swimming!"

And before I could think twice about the rush of frigid water that would flood my body, I dove in. Soon the three of us were playing tag, frolicking and laughing, diving and splashing, totally happy and carefree. I could imagine that Ted, watching us, would have been smiling. This is how he lived his life – he jumped into it. He lived it fully. In those precious moments of play with my grandchildren, I felt as if we were all One. Ted, me, Skye, Ian. One energy. One joyful experience of life.

The poet David Whyte writes about the importance of being willing to "hazard" ourselves in the world. Freedom comes from living at the frontier, at the edges of our life. Where that edge may be depends on what we have experienced so far on our journey. I was up against my edge – a small one but nevertheless an edge – that day in the swimming pool when I was reluctant to get my hair wet. It wouldn't have been an edge for many women, but it was for me.

When we make that choice to step into the unknown, we have to be willing to be vulnerable, to fail, to embarrass ourselves – to get our hair wet. But when we step off the comfortable path or venture to a depth that feels hazardous, like it might not hold our weight, like we might sink and drown, something amazing happens. When we move towards something worthwhile, the very *nature of what calls us* makes it possible for us to navigate that difficult terrain. The courage or inspiration that draws us to step off the safe and familiar path provides the resource that carries us safely across.

One horribly difficult night a couple of years after Ted died, I was invited to the wedding of a friend of mine. Weddings are hard for a widowed person, but this one was especially tough. It was held at the Cambridge Boat Club, the rowing club to which Ted had belonged and where we'd spent so many happy times. I'd never entered this building without Ted by my side.

That night, as I walked in alone, I felt the air saturated with Ted's presence, or rather, his absence. He was everywhere, but nowhere. I wandered upstairs and found, in the glass case, his photo alongside the trophy he had been awarded after completing that last, fatal race. I was flooded with memories of the many times we'd come here to watch the Head of the Charles rowing competition, or attend banquets honoring him and other rowers. And it was here that Ted and I took a series of ballroom dancing lessons. What fun we'd had. Remembering this, my feelings were all a jumble. A big part of me now hated this place. If he hadn't developed such a passion for rowing, he wouldn't be dead now!

I got through the dinner part of the evening with a frozen smile on my face, but when the dancing began, I was a wreck. Then, the couple I'd been chatting with joined all the other couples and walked hand in hand to the dance floor.

I felt adrift. I walked out onto the porch and watched the river silently flowing by, the very river that had given Ted such joy. I felt grateful when a friend of mine came out and visited with me for a while. By and by, I noticed a few people leaving, and I thought, *Now's my chance to get out of here.* But as I was preparing to make my getaway, I noticed a few people dancing to the Village People's hit song, "YMCA," and before I could let my fear talk me out of it, I walked onto the dance floor and joined in. Gradually, the music and movement helped the ache in my chest begin to dissipate. The band continued to play a few more songs that people could dance to without needing a partner. I was able to jump into the flow and rhythm of life – rather than just standing on the outside feeling left out. I actually had some fun, and left feeling enormously grateful that I'd not slunk out the door earlier.

Once I took that step out onto the dance floor, my courage and my love of dancing – which had gone away with Ted's death – revived enough to carry me forth. I was able to make a good time for myself.

I also found Stephen Levine's words helpful. *"Fear reminds us that we have come to our edge. We are about to enter unexplored territory."* In this sense, there is nothing wrong with feeling afraid. It simply means I am being given an opportunity to expand my personal boundaries.

I've had lots of these "opportunities." Several years after Ted died, someone from church who knew about the journey through grief I'd been going through asked me if I would lead a Sunday worship service. This included giving a sermon. A surge of anxiety rushed through me. My biggest fear in life has always been public speaking. This was a *big* edge for me. My mind flashed back to panic attacks I'd had in the past. I remembered many a time when, as I waited my turn to perform in front of others, my heart would suddenly take off and race uncontrollably. Panic would rise in my body like an enormous wave washing through me, and after dwelling for a while in my chest and throat, it would gradually fade away. I always feared I'd be called on to speak before my pounding heart could quiet itself. I feared I'd be a jabbering idiot, or that I'd simply stand there, paralyzed, with no words coming out.

But, I had come a long way since then. I'd begun to build a track record in my own mind of successful speaking experiences. In addition, I had been excited to share with the congregation some of the things that I'd found so amazing that happened after Ted's death – the rainbows, my dreams, the strange electrical phenomena and the other ways I'd felt Ted had made his presence known to me. I'd wanted to share some of what I'd gained spiritually along the way. (All of which I will elaborate on in the next sections.)

As I continued to struggle with whether to accept the invitation, Ted's voice came to me. "Do what *feels* scary, but what you know in your head to be quite safe." So I chose to listen to Ted, and I agreed to lead the service.

As you can imagine (or I wouldn't be telling you this story), the sermon turned out very well. As I think back now, part of what had carried me through was the very message I had shared with the congregation.

Every time I have pushed myself to step outside my comfort zone toward something of value, somehow I've found the resources to handle it. Or perhaps the source has found me. When I have taken these kinds of emotional risks, my sense of Ted's continuing presence carries my through. He *is* the wind beneath my wings.

Nature Works Its Healing Magic

"Stand still. The trees ahead and the bushes beside you
Are not lost. Wherever you are is called Here,
And you must treat it as a powerful stranger,
Must ask permission to know it and be known.
The forest breathes. Listen. It answers,
I have made this place around you.
If you leave it, you may come back again, saying Here.
No two branches are the same to Raven.
No two trees are the same to Wren.
If what a tree or a bush does is lost on you,
You are surely lost. Stand still. The forest knows
Where you are. You must let it find you."

David Wagoner
"Lost"

Ted dearly loved the natural world. He felt passionate about our need to take care of this precious earth. "We need each other," he would say. Ted and I enjoyed the outdoors in many ways. Sometimes we were active and playful as we camped, hiked and skied the mountainsides and paddled the rivers and ocean. At other times, we were more quiet and meditative. We owned a little cottage on Frye Island in Lake Sebago where we enjoyed sitting down at the point and gazing across the five mile expanse of water to the mountains in the west. Often we sat there in silence, taking in the sheer beauty of it all. I remember Ted remarking to me (and then later writing in his annual Christmas letter) about the serenity he felt there.

"Each night the sun disappears behind the mountains as the earth slowly rolls away. The water is in about the right place, cuddled in a fold in the earth's surface. It seems to belong there. The sky and the clouds are out there, again about where they're supposed to be. And though the sun drops down differently each night, it always does it about the way it is supposed to. Sometimes the wind is still and the water is a glazed mirror. At other times three-foot waves crash on the shore at our feet. Again, whatever the configuration of wind, waves, lake, shore, sky, sun, clouds and Earth, all the pieces seem to fit together. Nothing is out of place. Even time is moving at about the right rate. We feel connected with it all. We are a part of it. It is obvious that there is nothing we need to do. We sometimes wonder if this would all be here without our watching it. Certainly the serenity would vanish."

Sometimes we found nature to be therapeutic. One weekend, Ted and I went to an eco-psychology conference; it was a workshop designed to be healing for practitioners while offering techniques that we could take back to our work with our own patients. In one of the experiential exercises, the facilitator asked us to go out into nature and bring to mind an issue that we found troubling. Let the woods speak to us. I wandered around a bit and then found an old stump and sat down. I had been working to overcome my performance anxiety and feel more comfortable standing out and being seen. My way of surviving as a child was to disappear into the woodwork.

As I looked around, I noticed: a towering blue spruce standing erect and stately; a perky little dandelion peering cheerfully at the sky; a graceful birch with glistening white bark and delicate yellow-green foliage shimmering in the sunlight; and a tiny sprig of some young plant poking its way expectantly out of the earth. I was struck by how each of these growing green things, from the most massive to the most miniscule, proudly took its place on this earth. None of them apologized for existing. I walked out of the woods that day holding my head a little higher.

A few years after Ted died, I went out to California by myself to attend a friend's wedding. I was feeling particularly sad and lonely. I missed my husband acutely as I remembered our own wedding many years earlier. I thought to myself, *Perhaps nature can again perform its healing magic.*

As I left my hotel room one day, the sounds of the waves pounding in the distance drew me down to the waterfront. I sat on the beach, and the fresh ocean breeze and the warm sun on my face helped the tightness in my shoulders begin to relax. After a while, I got up and began to stroll down a little path. I took in the lush beauty. My attention was drawn to all the life around me. I soared for a while with the gulls that were riding currents of wind, and then every so often swooped down to the water for a tasty morsel. I scampered with the squirrels, playing hide and seek through the branches of the trees. I crawled with a tiny ant as he meandered his way through tall blades of grass and up and over clumps of dirt. I wondered what his experience was like. Did *he* know how to find his way home? Did *he* ever get lost?

I strolled along the path, deeper into the woods, found a place to sit and listened to the sounds of the forest. I became aware of layers of sound – a background hum of crickets, the ocean in the far off distance, the chirpings of various birds conversing with each other, the wind in the trees. It was as if I were listening to a symphony; so beautiful. I began to sense that there was something more beyond these sounds and sights. Something shined through these forms. A depth revealed itself. I felt a hidden harmony ~ you could even call it sacredness ~ in which I suddenly felt the connection between everything. Everything fit together.

Further along the path, I noticed an enormous spruce tree standing tall and erect. As I looked more closely at the top, I saw two tips reaching to the sky. Then I realized that this was not just one, but two trees growing so closely alongside each

other that they looked like one. This reminded me of similar pairs of evergreen trees I had found so remarkable in the Colorado mountains. I thought to myself, *Ted and I were like these two trees.* Over the years, our branches became so intertwined that you couldn't tell where one tree left off and the other began. Our trunks each grew sturdy and strong, gaining support from the other. When winter blizzards and fierce winds lashed our bodies, we stood tall. On first glance you might have seen just one magnificent tree and not realized that there were actually two of us...so completely had we merged.

When Ted died, it was like a vicious storm had come along and ripped one tree out of the ground leaving the other brutalized. The lonely tree was a wreck. One whole side of her was in shreds; she felt exposed and vulnerable to every passing storm.

While looking at the tree, I imagined the passing of time; the remaining tree, like me, struggled to survive. Courageously, she lived on – she had no other choice. She gained sustenance from the sun that warmed her branches and the gentle rain that fed her roots. She gained strength from the companionship of other trees nearby. In time, her limbs healed and new growth appeared. She grew in height and her foliage became lush and rich in color. She began to feel useful to birds that built their nests in her limbs and squirrels that scampered up and down her trunk and played amongst her branches.

And then I imagined some hikers coming along who remembered this tree from an earlier year and now noticed how strong and lovely she had become.

"What has happened to you?" they would ask the now healthy tree incredulously.

"Lots," she would reply. *"I had to make it on my own. I could not live in his shadow anymore; he was not there to hold me up. My broken places got stronger."* And then in a quiet voice she would ask them a question.

"Would you like to know a secret?" She would then confide, *"No one can see it, but I still have his roots with me. They're under the ground, and they give me my courage. His roots are wrapped all around and inside of mine. In fact, they're not his roots anymore, they're our roots."* I smiled at the story that I had imagined while on this little hike.

As I began to walk back to my hotel, I felt like something magical had happened to me. I had been taken out of my small, isolated, self-absorbed self and had once again been connected to the larger world. I smiled at people. They smiled back at me. I felt a certain kind of rightness with the world – life was flowing along and, like Ted had said, everything seemed to belong in its place, and was doing what it was supposed to.

Back in my room, I remembered the sea gulls soaring over the ocean, effortlessly gliding on the wind. If someone were to confine a bird in a small room, he would dart from side to side in a panic, banging against the walls and windows trying to escape. Ultimately, he'd become injured or exhaust himself. But if you were to open the window and release him into space, he would spread his wings and soar, relaxed and free. I had found a way that day to open my wings to the larger world. And in the process, I found I wasn't alone and I wasn't afraid. The painful reality that my husband is dead didn't go away, but the space around it had hugely expanded so that I could realize I am more than the pain within my heart. As I opened to the world, the pain shrank in comparison. My pain takes up only a small part of my life. It isn't my whole being.

My Valentine From Ted

"In your light I learned how to love.
In your radiance how to see beauty.
You dance inside my chest
Where no one sees you.
But sometimes I do
And that becomes my light."

Rumi
"The Essential Rumi"

One Valentine's Day, three or four years after Ted's death, I made a big decision. I took Ted's wedding band out of my jewelry box, put it into my purse and took it to the jewelers to have it melted down. I'd had the idea of making it into a heart-shaped pendant for a long time, but I'd been ambivalent about doing it. I hadn't wanted to destroy the integrity of his ring. This was probably another way of holding onto Ted – as if he would be coming back any day now and would want to know where his ring was.

I had imagined Ted's ring to be lonely lying by itself in the dark jewelry case – never to grace the hand of anyone again. I'd been wearing my wedding band on my right hand, but I hadn't known what to do with Ted's. It would have been silly for me at that point to begin wearing his ring on a chain around my neck – like a high school senior going steady. I had finally come to the realization that he was never going to come back to wear it. In fact, no one was ever going to wear his ring again. My two sons have wedding rings of their own and my grandsons will want their own someday, too.

I remembered what a joyful time we'd had back in 1968 shopping for our wedding rings and planning our future life together. We had ventured into a little jewelry store in Palo Alto and discovered a jeweler who could design and craft a pair of engraved wedding bands. What a magical day that had been for me – I was going to marry my prince charming!

This time, 38 years after picking the rings out together, I walked into a jewelry store alone. I explained to the jeweler what I had in mind. He showed me various styles of hearts he could make from Ted's ring. He explained that he'd create the design with his computer, then send Ted's ring off to be melted down and cast, and then he'd hand-shape it into its final lovely contours and add the sparkle of some little diamonds. As we talked about his inscribing the original words, "From Cindy with love to Ted, July 13, 1968" on the back, I began to feel the beginnings of tears swirling in my chest. I was finding it hard to let go of the ring and hand it over to the jeweler and say goodbye to it forever. I felt silly wanting to kiss it and squeeze it one last time. I was still trying to hold onto my composure when the jeweler smiled at me and spoke so kindly.

"I will make it beautiful for you."

I felt the rush. Here they came. The surge of tears rose in my chest, filled my throat and spilled out of my eyes. Nothing could stop the wave now – I just had to hold on while it washed through me. He waited patiently.

As the days went by, the perfect metaphor came to me. I was finally able to feel good about changing the shape of Ted's ring. I didn't destroy its integrity. The wedding band and I have both undergone the same process. We both have gone through a metamorphosis. Ted's wedding band endured intense heat, was melted down, pounded and hammered, shaped and re-shaped and emerged in a marvelous, new, dazzling form. The ring was transformed into a symbol of beauty and love. I too have been smashed and beaten, battered and pounded. Melted and reshaped. Reshaped again and again. Over time, I have become transformed. I have been expanded and deepened and softened as a person. Enduring the fury of grief has forever changed me.

Ted's ring, now a lovely heart, is a tangible expression of how I carry him in my heart. I have let go of the physical reality of Ted in my life, but his spirit, his essence, will be a part of me forever. And then, as an added gift, when I looked at my new heart-shaped pendant for the first time, I was astonished to see two graceful swans kissing!

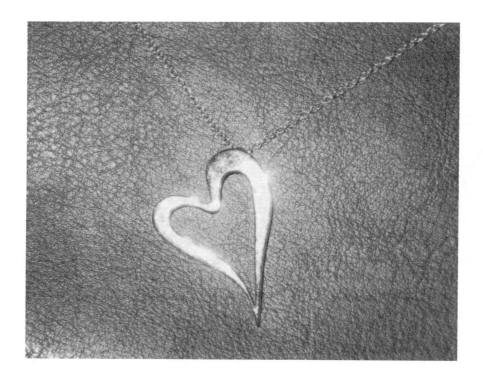

A Smorgasbord Of Survival Tips

"It's ok to just sit in your house and cry,
The walls hold in what you can't."

Unknown

- *"Allow the tears to come. They are nature's way of healing yourself. Just as when your skin is cut you bleed, when your heart is broken you need to cry."*
  Webb Brown

- Join a widow's support group. It helps to share your grief with others who know the devastation of losing someone beloved. <u>And</u> it helps to listen.

- Accept invitations from others with whom you can be real and talk about what you are going through. Decline those where you'll have to put on a happy face and make nice.

- Weekends and holidays are some of the most difficult times. Make a plan for how to get through them, rather than passively letting them happen to you. This gives you some sense of control. Arrange for at least one activity on the weekend. It can be helpful to change the way you celebrate holidays from the usual family tradition.

- Reach out to other widows and arrange to get together for lunch or dinner at least once a week. When you are feeling blue, pick up the phone and call a friend or another widow. The bottom line is – **reach out, rather than pull back from life.**

- Get involved in some kind of regular exercise: join a gym, find a regular walking partner, learn to play golf or tennis, join a hiking group or yoga class, swim. Physical activity releases endorphins and is a natural mood enhancer.

- Don't make any major or irrevocable decisions – selling your house or moving – until you have your feet on the ground in your new life and you know you won't regret it.

- It helps to rearrange the furniture, put in new plantings or buy new items for your home. In my case, I bought a new bedspread with matching scatter pillows as a way of moving ahead. Make changes to the household environment to suit your own needs. You may want to clean out his closet, workshop or study to make it into a space of your own. I also rotated my mattress. Crawling into my king size bed every night and lying in my own hollow imprint only further emphasized my aloneness.

- Start a journal. I found it helpful to put to paper the thoughts, feelings and experiences I was going through – and, yes, the small triumphs I had along the way. I suggest you <u>not</u> get a lovely book beautifully bound with fine stationary, because then you might feel inclined to filter your thoughts and write with your best penmanship and grammar. You want to be free to let it rip, freely expressing your anguish, self-pity and rage. Journal writing is a good way of externalizing your feelings. You will also feel encouraged when you look back and see your progress over time.

- Make a scrapbook, photo album or write the story of your marriage (as I did). Although it's bittersweet to revisit all those nostalgic memories again, and may bring a flood of tears from time to time, it is strangely comforting. The day will come when your sadness has lifted and you'll be left with the rich memories of your life together – which you can re-visit any time you want, just by opening the book.

- Take your wedding ring off, or move it to the other hand or re-fashion it into a piece of jewelry or another ring – if and when the time feels right.

- When hiring a repairman to fix your car, your washing machine, your roof – give him the impression you have a man in your life (husband, son or brother) who you will consult with after he's given you his estimate. You're less likely to be taken advantage of if they don't think you're a lone woman out fending for yourself. Also, get a second or third opinion – estimates can vary greatly.

- Get a handyman. If your husband was the handyman, it's easy to hire another one. It's not so easy to get another husband.

- Anniversaries, birthdays, holidays are hard. On my husband's birthday, I invited my grandchildren to roam around the house and find something of granddaddy's they might like to keep. On your birthday you might buy yourself something special, knowing your husband would say, "Honey, just do it." Light a candle or give a toast to your husband at celebratory family occasions. Keep your husband's memory alive within your family.

- Before engaging in sex, as awkward as it may be, you need to be sure that your new partner is not exposing you to any sexually transmitted diseases. If you think he has had other sexual partners, it is important that he has seen a doctor and had the necessary blood tests. You may be long past the time when you have to worry about pregnancy, but STDs can happen at any age.

- There is no timetable for grief. Don't listen to others when they say or infer that, "You should be over it by now."

Becoming Real

Rabbit asked Skin Horse, his friend in the nursery, about how to become Real. His friend said:

"Real is a thing that happens to you. When a child loves you for a long, long time, not just to play with, but REALLY loves you, then you become real."

"Does it hurt?" asked the Rabbit.

"Sometimes", said Skin Horse. "When you are Real, you don't mind being hurt".

"Does it happen all at once, like being wound up, he asked, or bit by bit?"

"It doesn't happen all at once, said the Skin Horse. You become. It takes a long time. That's why it doesn't often happen to people who break easily, or have sharp edges or who have to be carefully kept. Generally, by the time you are Real, most of your hair has been loved off, and your eyes drop out and you get loose in the joints and very shabby. But these things don't matter at all, because once you are Real, you can't be ugly, except to people who don't understand."

Margery Williams
The Velveteen Rabbit

If Ted had died earlier in my life, I would've had a much harder time of it. I know I would not have gone on to thrive. My achieving, needing-to-look-perfect, don't-let-anyone-see-your-weaknesses personality would have found it hard to accept help. I probably couldn't have admitted, even to myself, that I needed help. I certainly wouldn't have let anyone see my tears. Jacqueline Kennedy, with the steely, smiling brave front that she exhibited to the world, would have been my role model.

This brave front that I, too, showed the world earlier in my life has been called the *"false self,"* a term originally coined by psychoanalyst Donald Winnicott. It is one kind of mask that we all put on at an early age to cover our vulnerability. It protects us from the assaults of an unpredictable and sometimes frightening world.

When a baby is born, she arrives in the world naked and free of camouflage. She exists as pure being, living in the moment, spontaneous, open and free. This is her true or authentic self. She hasn't yet developed the confines of an ego. She isn't constantly seeking to anticipate other's expectations and modify her behavior to gain the approval of caretakers. My baby granddaughter doesn't fret over the past. *I should not have pooped in my diaper just when Mommy got my snowsuit on.* She doesn't worry about the future. *Will Mommy remember to come feed me tonight when I'm hungry?* She doesn't try to perform or achieve. *Tonight I'm going to be a good baby and sleep all through the night so Mommy can get some sleep.* She just is. And most of the time she is an utter delight.

But as babies grow and begin to crawl around, the civilizing process begins. Children can't be allowed to do whatever they want. They need to be said "No" to and taught how to behave; they need to be protected from the dangers of the world; they need to learn to think about the needs of others. Thus, the personality and ego become formed. The ego helps us differentiate ourselves from others: "This is *my* toy."

The ego gives us our sense of identity: "I am smart / pretty / strong."

A child finds a mask to help him survive. The more difficult a child's circumstances are, the more rigidly the mask is held in place. The more optimum a child's world is, the easier it is for his natural radiance and authentic self to shine through.

This brings to mind my earliest memory, an event that happened when I was about three years old. I remember seeing an open door and scampering out into the backyard, full of joy and exuberance. I had not a stitch of clothing on. The warm sun and gentle breeze must have felt good on my bare little body. How happy and carefree I felt! Then, all of a sudden, I felt this large form looming up behind me. My mother scooped me up in one big rush and whisked me back into the house where she scolded and paddled me.

"What a naughty girl! We *never* go outside without our clothes on! *Shame* on you!" Is it any wonder that, with an experience like this, I grew up to be compliant and inhibited?

Along the way, I discovered that as important as my ego has been (it helped me grow up and leave home), it also created separation. It is this sense of separation that creates suffering. No matter how healthy a personality we manage to develop, it still causes us to view the world in terms of *me* and *you, good* and *bad* – a world of duality. We are each the center of our own little universe. It's all about *me*, living in a world of *not-me's*. We see ourselves as the most important thing. The only trouble is, no one else agrees with us! Everybody *else* is saying *they* are the most important. We're all like little islands existing separately with no connection to the whole.

The reality is that even in the best of circumstances, our authentic self becomes buried under layers of protective armor. Our ego and personality develop in an attempt to cover the vulnerability and spontaneity that became unsafe to show the world. In addition to the false-self mask of the good little girl who is anxious to comply with the expectations of her parents, there are other masks children acquire as self-protective armor. One child who has been abused and feels weak and helpless dons the mask of the bully, or alternatively that of the victim. Another who felt she needed to over-achieve to impress people might put on the costume of a movie star's enviable looks to feel good about herself. Still others try to gain attention by becoming the "cry baby." the class clown, the rebel or the "know-it-all." Another, deciding to get her needs met by taking care of others, might put on the costume of a nurse (or social worker!). Which leads me to another story about how my personality became formed.

Creation of My Mask

The central, dominating factor that shaped my life and personality was my father's alcoholism. I dearly loved my daddy. He could be a lot of fun. I liked "rough housing" with him on the floor – riding on his back and playing horsey or balancing on his feet and flying like an airplane. I was happy when he took out his accordion to play for us, or took part in family rummy games, or went sledding with us or helped me with my homework. But there was his dark side, the side that scared me.

I have painful memories of his coming home from work. For the first hour he'd be fine, but then he'd start with his bourbon and rapidly deteriorate into a monster that could become mean, unpredictable and out of control. His appearance changed visibly – his eyes bugged out, he couldn't walk straight and he slurred his words. Sometimes he'd lose his temper and hit us or take off his belt to us. More often, it was my sister who was on the receiving end of his anger. Sally's frequent tantrums earned her the family nickname of "cry baby," so I learned from her how **not** to behave. I tried to be very, very good in order to become invisible and avoid his wrath.

My mother was not around in the evenings. My father's drinking made her nervous and she didn't know how to handle him. So she found a job in a drug store where she could work nights.

Starting from when I was ten years old, my mother left me in charge of taking care of my little sister and making dinner for the three of us. I always had my radar out. As I waited for my father to come in the front door, I sat on the couch with my heart pounding. How would he be? Was he sucking on a cough drop, did his eyes bug out, could he pronounce his words? The signs were instantly apparent to me. And then my heart just sank.

I felt like I was always holding my breath, not knowing what he'd do. A child will never forget when her daddy, whom she so dearly loves, threatens to "blow his brains out" with one of the guns he kept on the gun rack.

We never talked about his drinking to anyone, not even each other. To the world, I put on a smiley face. I learned to not show how I felt on the inside or let anyone know what living in our house was really like. But alone in my bed at night, I let the tears have their way. I buried my face in my pillow so no one could hear my sobs. I cried and cried until sleep finally rescued me. So often I said to myself: *Daddy, if you really loved me, you wouldn't drink.* I tried to get good grades in school and not misbehave so that he would be proud of me and love me. I hoped maybe this would stop him from drinking. I tried so hard to make him happy.

As a result of my hyper-vigilance to my father's moods, I became very sensitive to other people's feelings and needs. *But I was oblivious to my own.* In fact, if I could make someone else happy, then I would be happy myself.

So, I tried to be perfect. I felt terrible if I ever made a mistake. This resulted in my doing very well academically, and I got a lot of positive attention from my teachers. I came to feel that it was only by achieving that I was worth something. If only I had been able, at that young an age, to look into the mirror and see past the reflection of the sweet, good little girl. I would have caught a glimpse of the scared little child who desperately wanted her father and mother to love and value her for who she was – defects and all.

I had found my mask to help me survive. But I continued to wear it long after it had outgrown its usefulness. As masks go, the achieving, "good girl" facade was not a bad one to put on. Other people praised me, and my ego took pride in my successes. Although maintaining my false front helped me hide the shame I felt about my father's drunkenness, it took a lot of effort to keep trying to look perfect. And of course, in my mind, I always fell short. It never occurred to me to tell anyone, even my best girlfriend, that my father was an alcoholic. It wasn't in my repertoire to let anyone see the real me – the child whose feelings were so easily bruised, the child who never felt good enough.

A Hollow Victory

The years came and went. With my mask securely in place, I entered college at Colorado State University. Because I was scared I might fail, I worked very, very hard. To my astonishment I got straight A's that first quarter. And then I just kept it up. I joined a sorority and was elected to various honor societies, and in my senior year I was chosen to be the President of Panhellenic Council, the governing body of sororities.

When the end of the four years had come, I was sitting in the darkened auditorium at the All-School Honor Night. The climax of the evening approached: the tapping of the Pacemakers. The title "Pacemaker" was CSU's most prestigious honor, an award for excellence bestowed on ten seniors who had contributed the most in their four years at CSU. The lights had been dimmed as the hooded figure carrying his long scepter walked slowly around the room, up and down the aisles, looking for his chosen recipients. From the graduating class of 1,000 students, five women and five men were to be selected. The tension mounted. The spotlight followed the ghostly figure as he walked deliberately around the room.

Slowly he began to make his way in the direction where I was sitting with my friends. My heart began to pound as he stopped directly in front of me. Then, with a great flourish, he carefully lowered his scepter and tapped me lightly on the head. I could not believe this was happening. All eyes were on me as I stood up and made my way to the front of the auditorium and onto the stage.

As I stood in the spot light with the other nine chosen Pacemakers, the most surprising thing of all happened. *I felt absolutely nothing!* Nothing. I felt hollow inside. I was aware of the discrepancy between my head and heart that told me that I'd been selected to receive the *highest honor* that the university could bestow, and my heart – that felt *nothing*. They didn't match. You might be thinking I was just in a daze, and numb to my feelings. But I didn't feel elated the next day either. I just felt empty inside.

On some level, certainly not a conscious one, I must have realized that my "good girl," over-achieving personality mask was simply not working. I'd attained the most anyone could ever hope to accomplish in college, but it didn't make me feel any better about myself. I still felt defective. Actually, now I also felt like an imposter. The recognition by the outside world didn't match how I felt on the inside. So I must have been at a state of readiness when my life took a most remarkable turn.

My Mask Begins To Fall Away

As I continued with my schooling the next year by attending the University of Denver Graduate School of Social Work, two unexpected things happened. I no longer felt compelled to get A's. If a course interested me, I enjoyed studying and doing well. If the course bored me, like *Social Work* and *Public Policy*, I didn't need to "Ace" it. Gone was my compulsive need to achieve. I just needed to pass. Having received the Pacemaker Award in college, I came to realize that I was not going to find a sense of self-worth by being a high achiever. I'd have to look elsewhere.

Then I had the good fortune to be assigned to a woman named LaVerne Pritchett as my fieldwork supervisor. LaVerne, a lovely African American woman, had a wide, generous smile and eyes that sparkled with warmth and kindness. Before this time, I had never even had a conversation with a black person. As a small child, I had looked at people with dark skin with great curiosity; they looked so different from the world I knew. Growing up in the 1940s and '50s in middle-class Denver, I witnessed a fair amount of prejudice and racial discrimination. Very few, if any, Negro children attended North High School.

This new supervisor was the first person that was able to see through my facade to the real me. She was gifted in helping me to open up and take off my mask. My transformation began the first week of school, when LaVerne asked us to write our autobiographies. Something about her, perhaps her joyful presence or her authenticity, helped me to trust her. On some level I must have sensed that I was being given an opportunity, that she was opening the door to a new way of being. I decided to take a risk, and I walked through that door that LaVerne was holding open for me. As I wrote about my childhood, I held nothing back. I had never told a soul that my father was an alcoholic. Now I shared details that I had never revealed to anyone.

This began a transformative year in which LaVerne skillfully guided me on an inner journey to know and heal myself. LaVerne modeled openness and transparency as she shared personal aspects of herself that in turn caused me, over the course of the year, to gradually reveal deeper layers of myself. In the safety and loving warmth of her presence I learned to trust again. I discovered the magic of being real.

The process of becoming more transparent occurred outside my supervision as well. I made an invaluable discovery about how to make genuine friends. In the past, my way of getting people to like me was to try to impress them with what I had accomplished. Of course, without realizing it, all this did was to help set me apart from people. That certainly didn't help me feel less alone. During my years in grad school, my two roommates and I had many deep conversations lasting late into the night. As I shared some of the more intimate, vulnerable sides of my life, I made a shocking discovery. Not only did they not ridicule or laugh at me: they actually seemed to *understand and accept me*. Furthermore, I didn't feel alone! They had their own worries or similarly embarrassing stories to share. I began to feel I wasn't defective; I was simply *human*.

In retrospect, my last year of graduate school was one of the most transformative years of my life.

Sometimes I think of LaVerne as *Grace* – as in the dictionary definition of the word:

"Grace: Unmerited divine assistance given to us for our regeneration."

At the end of the year, I decided to bring these various parts of my life together. I wanted LaVerne to meet the parents I had talked so much about, and I wanted my mother and father to meet this supervisor I had spoken of with such admiration. So I invited LaVerne over for dinner at my parents' house. This was a stretch for me. Cooking a nice dinner was something I hadn't done much of. In the afternoon, my mother and father went out to do some errands and I got busy preparing the beef stroganoff. The recipe called for one clove of garlic, and so I started cutting garlic. I cut and I cut, and I cut and I cut. What a job! I was finally done and the dish was in the oven when my parents walked in the door. My mother immediately gasped.

"It reeks in here! What did you do?!"

I said the recipe called for a whole clove of garlic. She smiled.

"A clove is just one of those little things. You put in the whole head!"

It was too late to start over; LaVerne would be arriving soon. We frantically started picking out all the little bits of garlic that we could see. You can imagine the rest of the story. Everything worked out just fine. The stroganoff was edible (we served small portions) and we all had a good laugh. More importantly than how the stroganoff turned out, I felt happy and comfortable just being with these important people in my life. I felt like I could be myself.

As I thought about it later, I realized what a fitting conclusion this was to the end of my graduate school days. When I received my undergraduate degree, I was honored with the college's highest award, *but I felt nothing inside*. In contrast, when I concluded graduate school, I made a less than stellar dinner and could still feel terrific about myself. What a gift to learn that I didn't need to be perfect, I just needed to be myself.

Becoming More Real

After graduate school, I went off to California. It was there, at my first job as a professional social worker, that I met Ted. We never would have made it past the first date if I'd been my old self. If I hadn't been able to risk revealing the more vulnerable sides of myself, but had instead only tried to impress him with one thing or another, he never would've asked me out again. Actually, he made it easy to be real. When we walked into the local movie theatre, he smiled at me with those warm brown eyes.

My heart melted. I felt I could relax and be myself with him. The rest is history, as they say. Thirty-five years of wonderful history. Over those years, my husband and I came to know each other intimately. We became increasingly open and comfortable with each other – with all our warts and farts and various imperfections. As we each responded acceptingly of the other, we each became more accepting of ourselves. Fortunately, by the time I was facing a future without my beloved husband, I was in quite a different place than where I'd begun. Along the way I'd become Real, like the Velveteen Rabbit.

Grief Finishes the Job

The final lesson in becoming real was Ted's death. In the early days after he died, I felt the whole world was all happily ensconced in their marriages while I was singularly alone. The most painful part of being widowed was this sense of aloneness. I felt the isolation most palpably when I came home to the empty house, or sat by myself eating dinner, or drove myself to the airport, or when the stroke of midnight came on New Year's Eve, or when all the couples thronged to the dance floor at weddings, or when I crawled into my empty bed at night, or, or…

Immersed in self-pity, I'd think about how the entire world – even beyond the human world – seemed to have a buddy, or mate or be a part of a kindred group. Eating dinner by myself at the table, I looked into the back yard and watched a robin hopping through the grass never straying far from his fellow buddy robin, as if an invisible line connected them. I saw squirrels scampering playfully up and down the trees chasing each other. I thought about the tendency of most living creatures to group together – whether it's cows in a herd munching grass or ants marching in a line carrying huge loads to their anthills. *So, what am I doing sitting here alone?!* I thought. *It's against the natural order of things. It's not the way it's supposed to be.* It was this sense of apartness that was so painful.

I thought about how being a "widow" meant I was alone, uniquely alone. Every other role I'd ever been in – as a child, a wife, a mother, a grandmother – meant that I was part of a relationship...which also meant I was important to someone. But when I acquired the title of "widow," I was now defined as a wife *without* a husband. I was alone. Which meant nobody needed me. Which on a bad day translated to, *I am worthless.*

But then I said to myself: *You know, you do have a choice. You can immerse yourself in self-pity and feel sorry for yourself. Or you can open your eyes to the world around you. You can notice that you're not the only one who's suffering. You are not alone. Your ability to give to others, to connect to others has not disappeared!* When my friend comes to the door, I am grateful to share a cup of tea with her and talk about the real things that we are going through. Who the hell cares if I forgot to put on lipstick this morning or if I have dirty dishes in my sink?

Over the years of being married to Ted, my mask had become more transparent. More of my true self could shine through. But then, grief finished the job. Sorrow broke open my heart and opened me to a deeper layer of myself. Having lost the most important thing in the world, I came to realize what matters in life, and that is *love.* How important it is to be kind to each other!

She with the most toys, fanciest house, fewest wrinkles, most beautiful clothes – she does *not* win. Surface appearances stopped mattering so much to me. I realized I don't have to succumb to my ego's misguided attempts to help me feel good. When insecurity rears its ugly head, I don't have to hide in the shadows, and I don't have to find fault with someone else in order to feel good. When my prideful ego wants to gain other people's admiration, I don't have to show off and put myself in the spot light. I learned I have a choice. I can just watch these impulses arise and not act on them.

The Eastern traditions have given a name to this part of the self that notices the work of the ego - and that is the *witness*. Ram Dass, a well-known spiritual teacher, writes in *Be Love Now*:

> *"One of the first steps in getting free of the attachment to this ego idea is to develop a witness. We have thousands of me's, but there is one that is separate and watches all the other me's. It's on a different level of consciousness. It's not just another role...The witness place inside you is your centering device, your rudder."*

The witness part of self helps bring us back to our authentic self, to being real.

It's been said that becoming a widow can put us on the fast track to spiritual transformation. *"God enters through a wound,"* Llewellyn Vaughan-Lee wrote. Becoming a widow can separate us from the rest of the human race, or the pain we suffer can connect us to others in a deep and meaningful way. I learned to trade attention *from* others for connection *with* others. And this is truly wonderful.

Part III.

Mystical Encounters

"If I die, survive me with such sheer force
that you waken the furies of the pallid and the cold.
From south to south lift your indelible eyes,
from sun to sun dream through your singing mouth.
I don't want your laughter or your steps to waver,
I don't want my heritage of joy to die.
Don't call up my person. I am absent.
Live in my absence as if in a house.
Absence is a house so vast
that inside you will pass through its walls
and hang pictures on the air.
Absence is a house so transparent
that I, lifeless, will see you, living,
and if you suffer, my love, I will die again."

Pablo Neruda
"Sonnet XCIV"

Synchronicity – A Glimpse Into The Unknown

"No problem can be solved from the consciousness that created it."

Albert Einstein

Often, when I was in the depth of sorrow, my aching heart would cry out, *Oh Ted, I really, really miss you. Please send me some kind of a sign that you're still with me.* Since his death, a number of unusual things have happened that I believe speak to a dimension of reality that exists beyond what we can perceive with our five senses. I know that some would say that it is my wishful thinking that has caused me to give random events a special meaning. I do know that these coincidental events have comforted me and helped me feel not so alone. In the earlier pages of this book, I have mentioned many of these unusual occurrences which I'll briefly summarize.

The first strange happening was my saying, *"I love you,"* to Ted as he walked out the door to row in the race that took his life. This was not our customary farewell – <u>except</u> when one of us was going away on a more extended trip. Why I chose to tell him I loved him on that particular morning is a mystery.

Then, there was the double rainbow over the water where Ted had died and the numerous reports by my friends of rainbows they had seen at or around the time of his death (see chapter, *"Ted's Parting Gift"*). Since then, rainbows also seemed to appear at especially significant times on many of my trips. I was overjoyed in seeing a sliver of a rainbow in the far distance when standing at the top of the starkly beautiful sand dunes in the Sahara Desert; I saw another one while I gingerly traversed an elevated walkway high above the Amazon rainforest; and yet again a spectacular rainbow filled the sky after we came across a rowing regatta on a river in Thailand.

You could say that all this is coincidental, and maybe so. However, the sheer abundance of these unusual signs and the meaningful times of their occurrence around crucial events makes me wonder. For me, the synchronicity of the rainbows is part of the mystery. The rainbow is a fitting symbol for Ted, because in life, his radiant spirit overarched the many people whose lives he touched. I think of the rainbow as a bridge reaching out to connect me to unknown realms beyond this earthly plane. It is a promise of something more.

You may recall the story of the two bears my family and I observed ambling along on the outcropping of rocks high above timberline on Mt. Washington when we scattered Ted's ashes. Anyone whom I've asked that is familiar with alpine mountain country agrees that this was a strange occurrence – it is rare to see bears high above tree-line in the mountains. Native American tradition views the bear as both symbolic of strength, and also as a shamanic figure appearing in dreams and visions, teaching us the importance of opening oneself to communing with spirit. This powerful symbol is also befitting of Ted.

And then there was my experience on the Southwest Airlines flight just a couple of months after Ted died in which the person who sat next to me was a Buddhist therapist who works with dying people. At the end of our trip, I'd thanked her for our incredible conversation. She responded.

"I prayed I would sit next to someone who would find my presence helpful." I can't imagine that, while reading my book in my seat, I would have looked *that* broken-hearted to other boarding passengers. I like to think that the Buddhist teacher choosing to sit next to me is part of the Mystery. (Which is word I use when I refer to God, or a Power Greater than Oneself.)

I have not yet mentioned another whole series of unusual electrical phenomena that have also happened to me since Ted's death. These events were so extensive and baffling that I will discuss them in a separate chapter. Likewise, I have saved for a later section some of the interesting dreams I've had, and my visits to the mediums. All of these phenomena I believe reveal another dimension beyond our ordinary waking reality.

Many of us, at some point in our lives, have experienced certain coincidences so startling that they compel us to wonder: are these simply random happenings or is there a deeper significance to be found in their occurrence?

I have mentioned previously that Carl Jung coined the term "synchronicity" to describe meaningful coincidences. He wrote:

> *"Every now and then we encounter those confluences of circumstances so improbable that they seem to hint at a deeper purpose or design."*

To explain these events, he theorized:

> *"Whereas most visible phenomena in our world appear to occur in a linear cause-effect way, like dominos falling upon one another, synchronistic events are 'acausal,' in that they seem linked by deeper archetypal patterns rather than by linear forces."*

Naomi Rachel Remen, author of *Kitchen Table Wisdom*, expresses similar thoughts about synchronicity:

> *"Occasionally, events cluster in particular ways that give us a glimpse of the deeper structures of reality, and suggest that time and linear causality may not be the ultimate way in which the world is ordered. Synchronistic events point to the possibility of a hidden pattern underlying the events of the world."*

Out-of-the-ordinary events that defy an obvious explanation have intrigued people throughout history. More than a hundred years ago, William James, the renowned philosopher and professor of psychology at Harvard University, had a less-well-known side to his illustrious career: he was also fascinated by psychic phenomena, mediums and spirits. One of the founders and an early president of the American Society for Psychical Research, he devoted much of his life to discovering evidence for life beyond death. He was committed to separating the quackery from legitimate psychic phenomena, and determined that the Society adhere to rigorous standards of investigation. In an essay called *"The Confidences of a Psychical Researcher,"* he wrote:

> *"Out of my experience...one fixed conclusion dogmatically emerges, and that is this, that we with our lives are like islands in the sea, or like trees in the forest. The maple and the pine may whisper to each other with their leaves, and (the islands of) Conanicut and Newport hear each other's fog-horns. But the trees also commingle their roots in the darkness underground, and the islands also hang together through the ocean's bottom...Likewise our individual human lives appear separated by fences of our own making. But on a deeper level our many selves are joined together in a common reservoir of connection. Our "normal" consciousness is adapted to our external earthly environment. But the fence is weak in spots and occasionally influences from beyond leak in revealing our, otherwise unverifiable, common connection."*

These writings speak to me of the idea of a Oneness, an interconnectedness existing at a deeper level. We can choose to write off these synchronistic events as "just chance," or we can view them as Carl Jung explained, as "an eruption of meaning" in our lives. Each synchronicity constitutes a moment when the curtain is drawn back and we are offered a flash of insight into a vast drama. We may sense a regulating intelligence underlying the world, orchestrating all its elements within some grand symphony of meaning. At the very least, synchronistic happenings suggest that there is more going on than we realize. Not so many years ago, we knew nothing of radio waves and electricity – and now, though we can't see them, we don't doubt their existence. Likewise, I believe that one day, more invisible forces will be discovered that will shed light on these unusual happenings.

Sweet Dreams

"Dreams never come to tell you just what you already know."
Jeremy Taylor

I can't say my husband's premonition-like dream in which he foresaw his own demise was sweet in any way (see chapter, *"Should I have seen it coming?"*). I found it eerily fascinating, in retrospect. As you may recall, Ted awoke one morning, visibly shaken, and told me he'd just had an upsetting nightmare involving ambulances, fire engines and sirens.

Then, uncannily, just a few days later, he collapsed after rowing his last race. His body was pulled out of the water and, like in the dream, ambulances and sirens and fire engines arrived at the scene. I wonder now if his dream was a foreshadowing of that fateful day lying in wait for him down the road.

We've all heard incredible accounts of people who have had these precognitive dreams foretelling events that do later come to pass – like Abraham Lincoln's disturbing dream that contributed to his premonition that he would die in office. Doris Kearns Goodwin writes of it in *Team of Rivals*:

> *"There seemed to be a death-like stillness about me,"* Lincoln reported. *"Then I heard subdued sobs, as if a number of people were weeping.... I went from room to room; no living person was in sight, but the same mournful sounds of distress met me as I passed along.... Determined to find the cause of a state of things so mysterious and so shocking, I kept on until I arrived at the East Room, which I entered. There I met with a sickening surprise. Before me was a catafalque, on which rested a corpse wrapped in funeral vestments. Around it were stationed soldiers who were acting as guards; and there was a throng of people, some gazing mournfully upon the corpse, whose face was covered, others weeping pitifully. 'Who is dead in the White House?' I demanded of one of the soldiers. 'The President,' was his answer. 'He was killed by an assassin!'"*

I had my first dream of Ted just a month after he died. In the dream, I saw him standing there, his tall, lanky self, but not moving or saying anything. Then, from somewhere I couldn't see, word came to me that, although a part of him had been taken away, he wasn't gone. Part of him would always be with me. I was overjoyed. I felt like I'd been sent a message from another realm.

I was then reminded of another dream I'd had many years earlier, when Ted was in the hospital with a rare and serious disease of the blood coagulation system, called TTP (Thrombotic Thrombocytopenic Purpura.) One particular night when he was gravely ill, I had to say goodbye to him to go home and take care of our young children. The statistics regarding Ted's illness terrified me: one-third die; one-third suffer incapacitating complications, like strokes; and one-third fully recover.

That night, I had a remarkable dream in which Ted was walking down the street near our office. As I watched from across the street, I saw a wispy, almost ghost-like essence begin to swirl out of his body and float upward. I was horrified. But then it reversed directions and came back down again and was drawn back *into* his body. It was like his spirit was leaving his body but then changed its mind and returned. The next day when I went back to the hospital, I learned that Ted had nearly died that previous night.

Earlier in this book, I mentioned a couple of other dreams that spoke to me of the Mystery, of something *"beyond"* our earthly realm. Both of those dreams held the promise that, if I worked hard to get through my grief and learned from it, I would be taken to a new and better place.

The first was the dream about swinging from the end of a long rope (see chapter, *"My Mirror is Shattered"*). The message was: If I can do my part and push off from the ground, I will soar higher and higher, and be free like a bird. It came to me in the dream that I would be able to achieve this because Ted's spirit is always with me. He's the wind beneath my wings.

In the chapter, *"Letting Go of His Things,"* I told of a dream in which I repeatedly caught a ball and then ran up a long ramp. I did this over and over. I knew it was important to catch the ball in just the right way. Only then would I be rewarded and be allowed to run up the ramp.

These last two dreams remind me of the Biblical story of Jacob. As a young man, Jacob was forced to flee from his home and journey alone to a strange land. He was escaping his father, Isaac, and his brother, Esau, whom he had greatly angered. On his first night away from home, Jacob dreamed of a ladder, like a staircase, stretching from where he was out to eternity. In his dream, angels were coming and going up and down the long staircase. This dream was transformative for Jacob. He had a vision of something beyond himself that gave him courage and hope.

After my dreams, I felt the same way – that I was connected to something *beyond*. Robert Moss, well-known dream expert and author of *Conscious Dreaming*, wrote:

> *"A dream may indicate a transpersonal source that goes beyond the individuality of the dead person himself."*

In another dream, Ted suddenly appeared to be just standing there before me, and I felt overjoyed when I saw him. But as I approached him, he began to evaporate right before my eyes, like fog on a windshield disappearing as a blast of hot air hits it.

I reached for him, but he was gone. My hands came up empty. After I woke from the dream, I felt both elated and very sad.

Yet, as I've thought more about the dream, it seems that the message may be that Ted is still here; he's just not visible to me anymore. Like water turning to steam, his physical form has disappeared and become a different form of energy. His spirit is still present – he's with me, around me, and a part of me.

Along with these dreams (which I hold onto as messages from the spiritual realm) my nights have occasionally been blessed with other dreams of Ted: he shows up in a crowd; or is driving me in a car; he is sitting by my side at a wedding; he is making love to me in bed. Sometimes, the dreams convey a specific message, but often they simply say to me, *"I'm still with you, honey."* These dreams always make me happy in a sweet, poignant way.

The question of whether there is life after death has intrigued people since the beginning of time. Does our consciousness survive in some form or another? Do loved ones who have passed attempt to make contact with us after their death?

Inspired by the pioneering work of Elisabeth Kübler-Ross who devoted her life to working with the terminally ill, two researchers named Judy and Bill Guggenheim launched an extensive study of After Death Communication (ADC). They interviewed thousands of people who reported having experienced a communication with a deceased loved one. In their highly regarded book, *Hello from Heaven,* they share over 350 firsthand accounts. These after-death communications may take a variety of forms.

The most common way our departed loved ones reach out to us is through our dreams. These experts agree that there is a significant difference between an ordinary dream and a dream in which the person we've lost travels to visit us. An ordinary dream is jumbled and fragmented and may easily slip away and be forgotten, whereas a dream that is a true ADC is vividly clear and orderly and very memorable. These dreams of the departed may come to us to give us closure and to reassure us that all is well with them on the other side.

"Yea, though I walk through the valley of the shadow of death,
I fear no evil: For Thou Art With Me."
"Psalm 23"

Another Story Of Synchronicity

A few years before Ted's death, an equally inexplicable event had occurred. My sister Sally, after living an unhappy life, died a tortured death. Her greatest source of joy had been the time she spent at our grandparents' ranch in the high mountains of Colorado.

After her death, we decided to hold a modest memorial service for Sally at the ranch. On a crisp, clear fall day, our immediate family met in the backyard by the barn and walked down through the meadow to the river and gathered around a big blue spruce tree. This enormous tree had been just a baby itself when Sally and I were little tykes building sand castles at the river's edge while our grandfather fished nearby. We played some of Sally's favorite Elvis songs and reminisced about happier days. Then we scattered her ashes around the tree.

Some months after her death, I sold my half of the ranch, and Sally's children eventually decided they needed to sell the half that they'd inherited from her. A few weeks after completing the sale, we began preparing for an auction to dispose of the remaining household goods. This was a sad day for us because the ranch, which my grandparents had homesteaded more than a hundred years ago, was dear to our hearts. My father had grown up here, and Sally and I spent the happiest days of our childhoods roaming the meadows and playing down by the river. Later, I'd brought our own children and grandchildren to this ranch to enjoy many happy times.

On the momentous day of the auction, about a year after my sister's death, a couple of unusual incidents occurred that we've never been able to explain. The first happened early in the day as crowds of people swarmed in and around the abandoned ranch house. They were "like maggots come to feast on road kill," we imagined Sally could have remarked.

My cousin, Jeanie, glancing at the grove of cottonwoods near the house, noticed something strange moving near the house. She called out to Shannon, my niece, and told her that she'd seen something that looked like a whirlwind, or *dust devil* as they are sometimes called, swirling amongst the trees. They jokingly said maybe it was Sally watching over the auction, an event that would have been appalling to her.

Shannon, my sister's younger daughter, was the last to close up and leave the property at the end of the day. The auction company had already packed up and left, and the dozen or more cars, loaded up with newly purchased treasures, tools, antiques and just plain junk, had all driven off. It was a hard moment, the final leaving.

Shannon walked around the property one last time and revisited all her old childhood haunts. She walked through the ranch house permeated by layer upon layer of rich memories, and then peeked one final time into the bunkhouse, cow barn, ice and coal sheds, out-house, chicken house, pig pen, and blacksmith shop.

Shannon said her goodbyes and walked down to the river to sit for a few minutes under the huge spruce tree where we'd scattered her mother's ashes just a few weeks earlier. She placed a handful of daisies next to the memorial stone and talked to her mother about the momentous event that had just occurred. Selling the ranch was something Sally would never, ever, have agreed to. "Over my dead body!" she might have said.

As Shannon sat there, a bumblebee came buzzing around. Later, she told us that she said to herself, *If that bee stings me, I'll know that Mom is pissed.* The bee flew on.

By and by, Shannon left the river and walked back through the meadow saying her final farewell. Back at the ranch, she turned to take one last photograph, and as she lowered the camera she heard a rustling, swishing noise in the tall grass about six feet in front of her. Her first thought was that it might be a little animal scurrying in the weeds, but when she looked more carefully, she saw the grass swirling around in a circular movement. Then, to her utter amazement, she saw a swirling whirlwind about five feet tall rise out of the grass and move another few feet in front of her. There it stopped momentarily and hovered, spinning around, and then it finally swirled away from her. As this happened, Shannon exclaimed:

"Mom!"

She watched this whirlwind shape disperse as it headed down toward the river. Shannon said it was like her mom was saying, "I'm going fishing!" She had no doubt that it was her mother, and was greatly comforted by the experience. She felt her mom was saying goodbye, and also giving her blessing to let go of the ranch.

"She could have scared me," Shannon said of her mother. "But instead, she just wanted to let me know she was here and it was okay."

I should add that we had never before seen whirlwinds at the ranch. On the plains of Kansas and Nebraska, one might see these dust devils swirling across the open prairies, but not in the mountains of Colorado. Furthermore, the day had been perfectly calm with no wind at all. Just as the rainbows and the bears had been fitting symbols for Ted, we all agreed that a whirlwind would have been appropriate for Sally. She liked to stir up a commotion.

Spooky Electrical Events

"And if I go, while you're still here
know that I live on,
vibrating to a different measure
behind a thin veil you cannot see through.
You will not see me,
so you must have faith.
I wait for a the time when
we can soar together again,
both aware of each other.
Until then, live your life to its
fullest and when you need me,
just whisper my name in your heart,
...I will be there."

Emily Dickinson

Six months after Ted died, a series of eerie electrical events began to happen. They started with a dream I had:

Ted, Sandy and I had been sitting around a big table. Word came to us that there had been an electrical problem. Sandy got up and left to take care of the problem, and Ted came around and sat next to me. That was the dream.

I wrote about it in my journal and never thought anything more about it. Only in rereading my journal several years later did I discover how soon after this dream the first of many weird "electrical problems" began to occur. Three days after the dream, I borrowed a videocassette of *Truly, Madly, Deeply* from a friend. The story was about a woman whose husband died and then, to her delight, he came back to be with her in the form of a ghost. At a crucial part in the video, during the reading of a poem by Pablo Neruda, the picture portion of the movie stopped working, the screen went blank, but the audio continued on. The poem was about the need to go on living after the beloved has died. After the poem ended, the picture came back on and proceeded just fine.

At the time I wondered, was the tape defective or was something else going on? I so much wanted to believe that this was Ted's way of sending me a message, and like the man in the video, Ted was saying that he is still here with me. I felt comforted, and my mind was opened to possibility.

A year or two later, the skeptic in me decided to do a little investigation, and so I borrowed the same video from my friend and watched it again. This time it worked just fine, all the way through. Since there did not seem to be a mechanical problem, I chose to believe my earlier experience must have been foretelling of events to come.

A few days after the TV mishap, another very strange incident occurred that I wrote about in my journal. Prior to this, I had been having an especially hard time coping with being alone.

1/23/02 – 5:15 am. *Beep, beep, beep.* My bedroom alarm lurched me into another day, interrupting my deep sleep. Sleepily, I made my way through the darkness into the kitchen, where I flipped on the switch of my espresso maker and then I tumbled back into bed for another 6 minutes of doze time. When the alarm went off the second time and the hissing, steaming sounds called to me from the kitchen, I got up to get my coffee. I brought my cappuccino back to bed and read for half an hour, which was my usual routine before beginning my day. Then, at 5:45, I got up to take my shower and get ready for work. On my way to the bathroom, I glanced in the living room and discovered the floor lamp in the far corner of the room was on. *That's weird,* I thought. *That light wasn't shining when I got up to get my coffee a half-hour earlier.*

I knew for a fact that I hadn't turned it on the previous night. When I was home by myself in the evening, I never spent any time in the living room, and so I'd never turned that light on. Sometime during that last half hour while I had been reading in bed, the light had come on – by itself – or with a little help from my friend, Ted, perhaps? This particular lamp was one that I always turned on by a remote control device – in other words, by energy waves, not with an on/off switch.

If this phenomenon had just happened once, I would have written it off as a fluke. But on several other meaningful occasions, that same light came on "by itself." I found the lamp burning brightly one afternoon when I came home to get ready for a date – the first time in my new life when I was going to meet a man! The next time the living room light phenomenon happened was the week before the first anniversary of Ted's death. I had invited several friends to be with me on Frye Island on Lake Sebago. Here we lit candles, read poems, sang songs and ended by blowing bubbles at the "point" down by the water's edge that had been one of Ted's favorite spots. At the end of the weekend, when I returned to my house in Lexington, I was thrilled to find the living room light brightly shining.

A week later, on the one-year anniversary of Ted's death, my children came home and we revisited Mt. Washington and hiked up to that special spot on the high rocks where we'd scattered Ted's ashes. Karyn and I arrived home in Lexington late Sunday night. As we walked in the door, she asked me:

"Now where is that light Dad keeps turning on?"

We went into the living room and there it was – *on again*! At least this time I had a witness.

Of course, the idea that Ted's energy had been responsible for the living room light coming on did seem a bit bizarre. I tried to use logic and reasoning to understand this freaky event. I first checked the lamp and the remote control device to determine that they were not defective. Then I thought perhaps the neighbors had an instrument that turns on electrical lights remotely, and that they were responsible for it. I tested this theory by seeing how far I could step away from the lamp with my remote controller and still be able to turn it on. But it wouldn't work beyond the living room itself. Then I came up with another theory: perhaps a little mouse scampers across the floor, climbs up the bookcase to the top shelf where I keep the device. He puts his little paw on the control button and turns the light on across the room. Somehow, I didn't think that was a likely explanation either. Maybe once, perhaps, but not as many times as the light had come on.

In addition to the living room light, there were a number of other episodes electricity behaving strangely in our home. These anomalous events always seemed to happen at a time that was significant for me. I noticed that the nature of the unusual electrical phenomena changed over time from a light turning on by itself and staying on, to a light blinking on and off several times. It was as if someone had repeatedly flipped the switch of a light off and on, off and on, two or three times in quick succession. Usually, my first reaction was to think, *The light is about to burn out –* but then it would go back to being on, staying on, and operating just fine. Here are some examples of these unusual electrical occurrences taken from my journal.

7/10/04 – I'm approaching the third anniversary of Ted's death and I've been awash with grief. A very thoughtful card from a friend triggered an avalanche of tears. I cried and cried. Then I decided I was already so devastated that I might as well go for the gold. So I put on the tape of an interview our daughter, Sandy, had done with Ted a few years before he died. Hearing his voice for the first time since his death put me over the edge. His voice was so clear and present, almost as if he were sitting with me in the room. In tears, I begged him to please let me know somehow that he was still with me; to send me a sign. The next morning as I was cooking breakfast, the overhead kitchen lights went off and on three times in quick succession. I believe it was Ted saying, "I'm here, honey." I was so grateful. *Thank you, Ted.*

8/16/04 – I think I heard from Ted again! I've been taking care of Nathan and Kenny for the last few days. I was sitting here at the kitchen table while they were bouncing the ball in the hallway, when all of a sudden, the overhead Tiffany light at the kitchen table went off and on two or three times. At first I thought I was losing power, but none of the other lights were affected. After they blinked, they turned on again and shined as brightly as before. I didn't say anything about the lights to my grandsons – but strangely, almost immediately after the lights blinked, Nathan and Kenny began talking about Granddaddy and asked to see his bones. (They knew that after I scattered Ted's ashes I had saved a few fragments of his bones in a little dish in my china cabinet.)

6/10/06 – For my 65th birthday, Sandy and Karyn gave me the most wonderful celebration. I'd invited a dozen of my friends up to Frye Island for the weekend, and in the midst of my birthday dinner, as I sat surrounded by my friends, suddenly the lights over the dining room table went out and then came back on. My first thought was, *Oh no, we're losing the electricity.* But after they flickered back on again, they worked just fine. My next thought was, *Ted, you were here at my party, too. Thank you for a wonderful birthday gift.*

12/01/2008 – Earlier in the evening, I had taken Karyn and Kara to the airport in Manchester after a Thanksgiving visit. It was an exciting and celebratory time because they had just shared that they are going to become parents. After returning from the airport, I turned on the TV for a little while and watched "Love Songs of the '50s and '60s," and naturally thought about Ted. Then I went to the kitchen to make my bedtime cup of tea. As I was leaning against the counter waiting for the water to boil, the one recessed light above me suddenly started to blink. It flickered vigorously on and off three times in quick succession. The other five recessed lights that were on the same circuit were unaffected. As usual, my first thought was to wonder whether the bulb was about to burn out, but after the series of three flickers, it behaved normally. If it had burned out the next day I would have said it was on its way out. But I didn't have to replace that bulb for another five months. A skeptic might say it was just a power surge, but how can a power surge not affect all the lights that are on the same circuit? It had to be Ted's energy.

So, in addition to this coming to me in my dreams, I was beginning to believe that Ted might be sending me messages through the unusual patterns of electrical behavior in our home.

I was, therefore, particularly interested to learn while reading the Guggenheim's book, *Hello from Heaven,* that many people interviewed in their study had also reported *unusual electrical occurrences* after their loved one died! Examples of these phenomena included lights blinking on and off, radios and TVs being turned on, and electric clocks acting up.

Other forms of ADC are also common. Genevieve Ginsberg reports in *Widow to Widow* that a high percentage of widows – as many as 48 percent in one survey – say they have experienced the presence of their husband sometime in the early months of bereavement. For some, this may take a visual form, in which the deceased person makes an appearance. Others have reported sensing the presence, hearing the voice, feeling the physical touch, or smelling the fragrance of the loved one.

One explanation for this lies in knowing that everything is made up of energy and vibration – from a solid wooden table to the clouds passing overhead. Everything vibrates to its own unique frequency. Those who have passed are now a form of energy and they may be able to interfere with electrical currents and use their energy to make their presence known.

In the following example from *Hello from Heaven,* a hospice director in Maine named Gloria had an unexpected visitation the night her patient, Duane, died of complications related to AIDS. She sensed his presence and also experienced a light being turned on and off twice.

> *"I turned off the light to get into bed and started to feel that somebody was there. I knew instantly that it was Duane! It was a total experience of recognition. In that moment of shock, I had an intake of breath. Just when I did that, the light went on, then off – then on and off again! It wasn't just a flicker – it was like somebody had turned the switch. Then I picked up a sense of elation from Duane and the message that he was all right. It happened! What I experienced was as real to me as going out and getting in my car."*

I also learned that many people report ADCs in the form of rainbows, butterflies or birds. The grieving person intuitively recognizes these as messages from their loved one who continues to live in another dimension. Butterflies are the most common form of symbolic communication, followed by rainbows. The rainbow is one of mankind's oldest symbols of hope and eternal life.

Hello from Heaven relates the experience of Mindy, whose 7-month-old daughter died of sudden infant death syndrome.

> *"Before Kimberly was born, we painted a huge mural of a rainbow and sunshine on her wall. Her whole bedroom was decorated with rainbows. And a lot of the gifts she received had rainbows on them.*

Kimberly was our rainbow kid! Ever since she died, on her death date and on her birth date, there are rainbows here. It's sunny, it rains, the sun comes back out, and then there's a big rainbow in the sky! That's Kimberly's way of coming to us and reassuring us that there's life after death. Last year, on her death date, we went to her grave. As we were leaving the cemetery, a big rainbow appeared in the sky in the east. It gave us shivers and chills and brought tears to our eyes – and smiles too!"

I find it reassuring to learn that other people have been comforted by rainbows and unusual electrical happenings following the death of someone precious to them and found these comforting. Like myself, they felt their loved one was reaching out from another realm saying, *"I'm here, honey. I'm still with you."*

Messages From Ted

Seven months after Ted died, I drove to the historical town of Salem, home of the Salem Witch Trials and other spooky goings on, hot on the trail of finding my dead husband. I could hardly contain my excitement. A widow friend of mine had recently spoken enthusiastically about an experience she'd had visiting a medium – a psychic who makes contact with those who have passed. Being naturally curious and a bit adventurous, and so much wanting to believe that some part of Ted still lived on, I was eager to have a meeting with the medium. *So, what's the worst thing that can happen?* I thought. *Nothing; I will have spent a few dollars and nothing will come through. I can live with that. I won't be any further behind than I am now. Except a few bucks. And I waste a lot of money on cappuccinos, anyway.*

I didn't tell many of my friends what I was up to, exploring the world of the paranormal. I could imagine them saying, "Cindy seems to have really gone off the deep end. Poor woman, and we always thought she had her head on straight. This grief must be getting to her."

Kevin Coan

I talked to Ted all the way up to Salem,. "Please honey, I need to hear from you. Please come through for me, let me know you're still with me."

I arrived in Salem, and located the medium's condo down by the waterfront. When I nervously rang the bell, I think I was half expecting some long-haired, pony-tailed guy in swishy robes to usher me in to a darkened room with the odor of incense hanging in the air and a crystal ball on the table. But I was greatly relieved to find Kevin to be an ordinary-looking young man with a crew cut, a friendly handshake and a warm smile. As I sat on the couch across from him, I glanced around and found his place also refreshingly normal – modestly furnished with a lot of books on the shelves but few decorations or touches of domesticity. I surmised a bachelor pad. I relaxed a bit, set up my tape recorder and we began.

A couple of hours later when I emerged from Kevin's house, my heart was bursting with joy. I drove to a nearby beach where I could sit by the ocean and absorb the impact of the experience. I felt nearly convinced that Ted was still with me.

A few months later, on the first anniversary of Ted's death, I went back for another reading with Kevin; this time Karyn and Brett joined me. They were curious to see for themselves what I had talked about so enthusiastically. Here are a few highlights from both of these sessions with Kevin. The thoughts I had in response to his reading are in parentheses, but I didn't share these with Kevin.

Kevin Coan: "I see a problem in his neck or chest area. He had a block in his throat, he's aware of something in his throat at his passing. His death was painless. It was a very fast, quick passing. One

128

minute here, next minute, boom, 'I'm gone.'" *(Ted might have felt the water flooding his throat and lungs as he was trapped hanging upside down with his feet clamped to his capsized boat. Or, Kevin may have been referring to the tube that the paramedics inserted in his throat when they tried to save him – the doctor told me that Ted still had a weak pulse as they drove him to the hospital in the ambulance, so he may have been aware of that tube in his throat.)*

"He had an interest in boats. He had a small boat. I see boat memorabilia in a room that he spent a lot of time in. *(Along with Ted's passion for rowing, we owned a couple of kayaks and a small motorboat. And our study does have a lot of photos of him rowing.)*

"He's a little bit on the analytical side, extremely intelligent. I see him teaching, or consulting, going to conferences affiliated with Harvard. There is something in your house that has Harvard on it. Did he ever publish something in the *New England Journal of Medicine?"* *(Ted did go to Harvard and was affiliated with Harvard in later years. We have two Harvard chairs and other things with Harvard on it. Although he didn't publish in that particular journal, he did write professional articles and was published.)*

"He was writing something when he died – but he'd gotten away from it, and didn't get to finish it." *(So true. He was in the middle of writing a book about what he'd learned from his patients, his colleagues and his friends, but he kept getting distracted and never finished it.)*

"He had an easy-going nature, he didn't sweat the small stuff. Sometimes people took advantage of his easy-going nature." *(Yes, Ted was easily drawn into investing in small start-up companies with some of his friends. With one exception, they have all gone belly up – the companies, that is; I don't know how his friends are faring.)*

"There are rainbows over water." *(Referring, of course, to the double rainbow over the river where Ted had gone down.)* "There are rainbows at your house that are not real." *(I have several crystals hanging in my kitchen window that cast rainbow reflections all over the walls when the morning sun shines in.)*

Other details about Ted that Kevin spoke of were his liking the outdoors, his being quite fit, Ted's ties on a door knob, a golden retriever dog who had passed who was with Ted, my not having gotten rid of any of Ted's things – all of which were true. Kevin also relayed several other specific bits of information about other family members, such as a conversation between Brett and his wife: "You were thinking about getting your baby daughter's ears pierced;" and another conversation between Karyn, Brett and myself that we'd had on the way to our session with Kevin: "Karyn, you are thinking about having your kitchen sink replaced;" comments about my grandmother: "She thought it was important for little girls to speak good English;" and, "She was on the ranch for a long time, never wanted to leave, wanted to die there;" and thoughts about my worries concerning Karyn's migraine headaches. These specific bits of information were to give us evidence that Ted is with us in our everyday lives.

When my children and I left the session with Kevin, we were thrilled beyond our wildest expectations. Even Brett, the more skeptical one of us, had to admit something was going on. How could Kevin have known all that he knew, and with such a high degree of accuracy? He relayed so many specific, unique-to-us details about our lives and about Ted that would have been impossible to learn by any research that he could have done. We had been careful to not be forthcoming in our responses and to try to sit impassively and just listen.

Afterwards, I typed out a transcript of these two sessions with Kevin and then rated each of his comments for accuracy. Were Kevin's statements true, maybe true, or not true? I found that there was a 76% rate of accuracy for being true and an 87% rate of accuracy for being true or maybe true.

You'd think that after having had these two remarkable experiences with Kevin, my curiosity would have been satisfied and any doubts erased. But there is always a small part of myself that remains skeptical.

Every now and then, I have needed another infusion to renew my belief that consciousness *does* continue in some fashion after we die and that Ted is still with me.

Over a period of several years I have visited a number of different mediums, and have found a huge variation in the quality of the readings I've received. Some have been extremely powerful experiences, and some have been real busts from which I walked away feeling enormously let down and disappointed.

There are a lot of people who call themselves mediums but who merely do "cold" readings; they speak in generalities – "He sends you his love," or "He will be there to meet you when you pass" – or they tailor their words in response to what they pick up by watching their clients' verbal and non-verbal cues. However, there are also some excellent, gifted psychics who, I believe, do make contact with the other side. These mediums usually cost more money and have long waiting lists, but I have found that they are absolutely worth it. Some of the good ones that I have visited, in addition to Kevin Coan, are John Holland, George Anderson and Suzanne Northrop.

While we're on a roll – maybe it's just your eyes that are rolling – I'd like to tell you a little about some of the other experiences I've had with mediums.

John Holland

On March 24, 2005, I drove up to Portsmouth, N.H., to attend a small group sitting with John Holland. I was thrilled to have a reading with John who is highly regarded in the field of psychic mediums. A receptionist seated the eight of us in a semi-circle, and we sat anxiously waiting for John to enter. I liked this small group format because, in addition to being less expensive, I found it fascinating to hear other people's readings and see how valid they seemed to be for them – which gave further credence to my own reading. We didn't talk much among ourselves but were all probably taking stock of each other. Finally John walked in and seated himself on a stool in front of our group – a handsome young man (anybody under the age of 50 is young to me) with a down-to-earth manner and a generous smile.

John began by telling us what to expect and how to have a positive experience. He said it was important to keep an open mind during the process.

"Be open to whoever is trying to come through and the messages they bring. I cannot guarantee you will hear from the person you want. The persons who come through are not going to predict the future or tell you how to live your life. The information that I bring you is meant to be evidentiary, to show evidence that spirit or consciousness continues after death of the body and that our loved ones who have passed are still around us."

He asked us to simply listen and not give him any information or ask leading questions. We were to respond only yes or no to validate the information we would be receiving. Then John closed his eyes for two or three minutes and appeared to be meditating or tuning to some other dimension. He had explained earlier that he raises his energy level and the people who have passed lower their energy to make a connection. We all sat quietly. I kept saying over and over to myself, *Oh please let me hear from you, Ted. Please let me know you're with me!*

When John opened his eyes he began going around our circle of eight, not in any particular order, speaking about fifteen minutes with each of us. First he went to a man and then to the women next to him. I watched in fascination as each of these people seemed to be nodding and finding what John was telling them meaningful. Then he turned to me. The information conveyed by John came through in bits and pieces as he was picking it up from "spirit," as he called it. He jumped around from one topic to another, so in an effort to clearly summarize what John said that day, I have organized his comments in a more coherent order according to the subject.

When John centered on me, he looked me in the eye, put the palms of his hands together and pointed his index fingers straight at me speaking assertively.

"Drowning. Your husband passed by drowning." *(He paused a moment and seemed to be listening and putting his attention on something inaudible and invisible to me.)*

"It was in fresh water, not the ocean. He was the only one who passed. There was an accident with your husband's passing. He's telling me, 'I screwed up.' He's taking some responsibility for passing, but it wasn't a suicide." *(As John spoke I kept my face as impassive as I could. I tried not to show any reaction although I was stunned. These words, 'I screwed up,' were the very words Ted would have used to express his regret for having made the fatal errors in judgment that day in preparing for the race.)*

John went on, "He was always on the water. He is saying, 'If I was gonna' go, I would go this way.' He had a premonition about his passing. *(That scary dream Ted had a few days before his death about ambulances and fire engines.)* "He knew somehow he was going: he set things up for you beforehand. He was quite proud of his boating, his rowing. There's a picture of him with his boat. I'm seeing a person doing it, the daughter who is single." *(Karyn, who was single at the time, was out kayaking the day he died.)*

"He is honoring what you did with the funeral service. He loved it. There were two locations, the scattering of the ashes." *(By now tears were rolling down my face; so much for being impassive. At least I wasn't providing John any information. I only responded "yes" or" no" to his comments.)*

"He was a nice guy, lots of friends... a heart of gold with this man. You were best of friends with your husband. You were married for quite a while. He's talking about the chain – something about a chain. I'm seeing Feb. 14, a heart connection, or February is significant. Your husband saw you manipulate the ring, adjust the stone." *(Referring to how on Valentine's Day, I had Ted's wedding band melted down, reshaped into a heart, added a small diamond and had it made it into a necklace that I wear on a chain around my neck.)*

"You still have the beach house. He loves that it is still in the family." *(Sandy and Jim bought our cottage at Frye Island on Sebago Lake from us.)* "Something about a tree, was there a tree planted in his honor?" *(Referring to the Granddaddy tree that Ted so dearly loved and around which I scattered some of his ashes.)* "He's showing all the books, a smart man. He's showing signs to you that he is around. You dream of him; memories of the Grand Canyon." *(One summer we'd ridden mules with Karyn and Brett to the bottom of the Grand Canyon.)* "Ted's friend Jack is with him." *(Jack Cole, a friend of ours had passed a couple of years earlier.)*

"I'm seeing a low-hanging beam in a previous house. Did you build your house? There was a misplaced beam." *(We did build a house and there was a beam that greatly upset Ted. The contractor had installed it too low and nothing could be done to change it, because it was supporting the whole house.)*

As I drove home from this small group reading, I was elated; overjoyed. I felt convinced that John had connected with Ted's spirit. I said to myself, *There's no way he could have found out this information by googling me or Ted.* In fact, there was one point that John got incorrectly, and it was when he asked, "Was he a businessman or attorney?"

"No," I had answered. John never did get that Ted was a psychiatrist, a doctor. If John had gained his information from the internet, that's the first thing he would have learned. Ted was always referred to as Theodore I. Anderson, M.D. in any publication by or about him. So even this "miss," as they call it, helped to validate John's authenticity in my mind.

Later, at home, I itemized all John's comments in the fifteen minutes he spent with me. I found that out of the 52 items, only 7 were not right or had no meaning to me. That is an 87 percent accuracy rate, which I found astonishing.

The next medium I visited gave a very different kind of reading.

George Anderson

The day had finally arrived for my appointment with the legendary George Anderson. For many months, I'd been waiting with great anticipation for this day because George had the reputation of being one of the world's greatest living mediums. I found it interesting to learn as I read about John Holland and George Anderson, that each had suffered a head trauma earlier in life. John had nearly died in a car accident when he was 20 years old. In *Spirit Whisperer, Chronicles of a Medium*, he writes:

> *"After the accident, the psychic abilities I'd experienced as a child, the same ones I'd pushed away at a very young age, were back now again, but this time they were a hundred times stronger."*

Similarly, when George Anderson was six years old, he suffered a near fatal attack of encephalomyelitis. Since then, he has been able to communicate with souls who have passed on. Medical professionals think that perhaps a re-wiring of their brains has occurred allowing them to connect with the very electromagnetic energy those who have died use to communicate with *us*.

For my appointment with George, I traveled to Long Island with a friend who was hoping to hear from his dead wife. We located the hotel where our reading would take place and found our way to a small conference room. We gave George's secretary our first names, found a seat in the circle of chairs, set up our tape recorders, and waited. None of us said very much, but I could feel the tension and anticipation rippling around the room.

Finally, George made his appearance. He looked quite ordinary (which apparently has been important to me), a slightly built man with a mustache, maybe 50 or 55. I can't remember the details of his appearance because he was so unremarkable.

George went in order, more or less, around the room. My excitement kept building. When he came to me, he started right off with:

"I have a man coming through, states that he is family." (My heart picked up a beat.) "He passed relatively young." (I said, "No" because Ted wasn't young.) George tried again: "Young by today's standards." *(Again, I said, "No" because as I was only 63 at the time of this reading. To die at 70 seemed old to me. I was beginning to feel disappointed, because I really expected to hear from Ted.)*

George moved on with other information for me. "Another man is coming forward, states he is your dad. His parents are with him. Also a lady comes forward states she is your mom." *(I was trying to shift gears and be receptive to the direction this was going and these other family members George was bringing in.)*

"Your mom draws close to you from over there – your mom admits she wasn't the happiest person on earth. She admits she was a sad, lonely woman who was sick at heart when she was here. She had tremendous emotional struggles. You didn't grow up in a Donna Reed-type home. Your mom apologizes for this, saying it was a very abandoning situation. You tried to get close to her, but she backed off." Then George talks about my dad saying, "He feels he kind of abandoned you, too. He acknowledges a drinking problem. It was embarrassing growing up. You didn't know what kind of state he'd be in. He didn't realize this could be humiliating for you. You didn't want to have friends over. Like your mother, he wasn't very happy and was trying to make things better but it also made things worse. In many ways, you were kind of like an orphan. You definitely came from an insecure, unsettled home." *(George's description of my father and mother was absolutely true – stunning. My father was an alcoholic, which was difficult for my mother. She was very upset by the situation and didn't know how to deal with him. She was an anxious, insecure and lonely person and not able to be very available to my sister and me. How could George know this, I wondered? He must be picking this up from Ted. I was still anxiously waiting to hear from Ted, but George goes on with more startling revelations.)*

"Also, two grandparents reach out to you closely. Grandmother embraces you with love, and if I didn't know better, I'd say she was your mom, because like when you were with her you were in a secure loving situation." *(I've often said those very words:* "My grandmother was more like a mother to me than my own mother.")*

"Unfortunately, your parents put a tossed salad in front of you, meaning as a child you were tossed around. But at least when you were with your grandmother you felt safe and secure and you also felt loved and wanted. Your grandmother states that when you were with her you could get a good night's rest, but when you were with your parents it was frightening for you as a child. Your grandma states she was glad she could always make you feel like you were wanted and that you were loved. As much as you feel she was a joy in your life, she wants to make sure that you understand that you were a tremendous joy in her life. That it certainly works both ways. You have not had the easiest life, but you've had a very fulfilling life. You've come a long ways, baby. She's proud of how you've achieved. Your grandmother embraces you with love and she is with you like a guardian angel. You've had a hard life and at times you might have been hardened by it, but she says you're still a sensitive person." *(My heart is bursting – George is so right. My grandmother meant life itself to me. She made all the difference. When I was at the ranch with my grandparents, I could relax and play and be a child, I could be happy.)*

And then moving on, "Also, your parents brought in a sister but who's passed on. She admits she could be a tough nut to crack. She wasn't the happiest person, highly emotional, very sad and also very lonely. She admits she wanted to pass on. She wanted out. She says, don't misunderstand this, but she contributed to ending her life. But she didn't kill herself." *(Again George was amazingly right. My sister did actively contribute to ending her life; she drank herself to death and passed when she was only 55 years old. Sally was very temperamental and could easily flare up in anger. She resisted all my efforts to get her to stop drinking or go to AA. Definitely, 'a tough nut to crack.')*

I could sense that George was beginning to wind down and was getting ready to go to someone else. As profound as this reading had been to this point, I still wanted to hear from Ted. So I decided I'd better speak up and say something.

I asked, "Can you go back to the man who passed young?"

"If he's still around. If you don't acknowledge it, they think things are wrong and they just back away. Yes, he was saying he passed relatively young. You seemed confused by it, and that I wasn't correct, and so they're inclined to back away. They feel you don't understand. Yes, he puts a heart in front of you – do you understand?"

My heart begins to surge.

"Yes, he says he's your sweetheart, but romantically. He states he was your husband. In the beginning he was building in that direction, but when you didn't react he cuts me off and walks away."

"Also, I don't understand it, but he puts the letter J in front of you. Understand?" (I said, 'No,' *but Ted may have been referring to Judy, his first wife who had passed before we met.*)

"I leave it with you. He comes to you in friendship. You did love each other and you were good pals. Certainly, like your grandmother, this was another joy in your life. He also has a wise-guy sense of humor. He made a wise crack, saying, 'Yeah, I'm such a joy in your life, she didn't even know who I was!' (Laughter)".

"Again he says you're friends. He can kid with you like that. One thing he does state. He's glad he passed before you. You're not exactly the merry widow, but he wouldn't have done well with it the other way around." *(Many times Ted had said, "I get to go first next time." Judy's death had been so difficult for him; he didn't want to have to go through that again.)*

"He admits he had a rough time prior to his passing, but in silence because he says he goes rather quickly. He says in essence he kind of drops dead. But he wasn't feeling right before, but he didn't say anything about it. He was just going with the flow. So he's kind of suffering in silence and doesn't feel right, but he says it was his time to pass and it couldn't have been prevented. He says he was feeling tired and out of sorts but he kept it to himself. Doesn't whine about it or make an issue of it." *(The night before the fatal race, Ted had been very tense, asking me to massage his shoulders and neck with the vibrator, something he'd never asked for before. Also, some rowing friends of his who talked with him the day before the race, later told me that he wasn't himself.)*

"He states he's always very near to you like a guardian angel. In saying this he could've passed at 80, but it's like I'm talking to someone much younger. There's that youthfulness about him. That bright outlook that's significant to his personality. That's why he came forward like this. He says you'd recognize him as being like that. He has a good sense of humor. He's fun to be with. Also, I heard the name Jack too, but connected with him. Jack is there with him." *(Jack Cole was a friend of his who had died two years earlier.)*

"Your husband does thank you for a very happy life with him. Glad things worked out the best for us, considering your origins. He just wants to make sure you know you could not have saved him. It was his time to pass on. And as far as he's concerned that was a happy passing. He didn't want to be a burden to his family. As he states, 'If I can't live a normal life, I don't want to stick around.' So to just literally drop dead, that's the way to go. His time comes, and his system shuts down and he withdraws. He also calls out to family so that everyone is acknowledged even if they're not called out by roll call."

"Don't correct me, but it sounds like I heard the name, Ted." ("That's his name!" I exclaim.) "Oh, because I wasn't sure if I heard Ed or Ted. At first I heard Ed and I was about to say it but then he said, 'No, say Ted.' That's why I said to you don't correct me because if Ted is wrong then Ed is correct. But he corrected it before I could open my mouth, so I'm glad I said Ted. His name is actually Ted with a T." *(Tears are streaming down my face – my heart is about to burst with happiness.)*

"He also extends white roses to you and pink roses. White is anniversary roses, pink for when you met, not the event of marriage. This is from Ted with love. He does have that wise guy sense of humor. He keeps kidding me. He says it's a good thing you mentioned it again, because he says, 'I was here in the beginning and I was busting my chops, punching a hole into this dimension and you didn't know who the hell I am. All that made my night." He says, "This is Ted, embracing you with love. A young guy at heart. He says just so you know you're not alone and that he's with you in a loving way, reaching out with love. He's going to pull back now so some other souls can come in. I'm just glad you said something, but you didn't call him by name, and he heard you and pushed back in again. I like his personality. He's fun."

I was elated. My heart was overflowing with joy. I had no doubt in my mind that George had been connecting with Ted's spirit. I clicked off my tape recorder, happy I'd been able to record this so I could be sure my ears and memory were not playing tricks on me. I walked out of there with a sense of certainty that life does go on and that Ted is still with me.

As I look back, it seemed that the sheer abundance and variety of synchronistic events that had happened since Ted's death were his way of reaching out to me. I grabbed onto them like lifelines of hope. They seemed to contain a secret; if I could just find the right key, I would be reunited with the man I love.

Attempts To Understand Paranormal Events

I wondered about what to make of these extraordinary events - my unusual dreams, the strange behavior of electrical lights at meaningful times and the messages from mediums. I sought answers in various books written about the study of consciousness.

Among the authors I read was one Lawrence LeShan, a Ph.D. research psychologist from the University of Chicago. A senior member of the American Psychological Association and past president of the Association for Humanistic Psychology, Le Shan was extremely skeptical about the world of the paranormal. So he set out to study telepathy, precognition, clairvoyance, deathbed apparitions, and communication with the dead. He intended to substantiate that these claims were ridiculous. In his book, *The Medium, the Mystic, and the Physicist,* Le Shan confessed,

> *"I asked myself what had fooled these people I so much respected into believing such obvious nonsense? To find the answer to this question, I looked at the data. This is a mistake you must never make if you wish to hold onto your beliefs and prejudices. The data were tighter than a drumhead. From dozens of laboratories and people of otherwise unquestionable probity came reports of experiments and of carefully investigated incidents that clearly revealed the existence of the phenomena I had so confidently derided."*

LeShan then began working with Eileen Garrett, a well-known, reputable psychic, in order to understand how the paranormal works. He wondered how it was possible for someone to know of things so separated from them in time and space and that they could not have known about using their ordinary senses. He learned that psychics are able to shift their awareness to another way of perceiving the world. They shift from the ordinary way of looking at reality, which is to focus on the separate, unique and individual aspects of things, to an awareness of the unity of all things and their relationship to the whole. LeShan tells of Mrs. Willett, a British psychic, who wrote,

> *"It is heavenly to be out of myself – when I'm everything and everything else is me."*

The ordinary way of gaining information about something is through our five senses and to interpret this data using the intellect. This is the *Sensory Reality* view. However, the psychic's way of gaining information is to accept the "Oneness" of everything. As LeShan puts it:

"In the way the world works, as seen in the Clairvoyant Reality, you and I are really 'One.' We are part of the total 'One' that makes up the entire cosmos. If I know that this is true and am reacting to you as if this were true, then - being 'one' - there is nothing to bar information exchange between us. So to speak, nothing can come between a thing and itself. From the viewpoint of the Clairvoyant Reality we simply have information circulating inside one thing. But when the same phenomena is observed from the Sensory Reality viewpoint it will be called telepathy."

LeShan went on to explore the world view of another group of people, those interested in mysticism. The teachings of famous mystics from ancient to modern times (the Buddha, Rumi, Meister Eckhart, St. John of the Cross, Kabir, Dogen, Ramakrishna, Eckhart Tolle, Deepak Chopra, etc.) show a marked similarity in beliefs. They also show a close resemblance to the psychics in the manner in which they access the paranormal. They see a fundamental unity to all things. All things are connected. All is One. During meditation, mystics try to go beyond the thinking mind and the five senses to experience the Oneness, the *Ground of Being* out of which all forms arise.

LeShan concludes:

"The whole multiplicity of things which comprise the universe are identical with one another and therefore constitute only one thing, a pure unity. The Unity, the One... is a central experience and the central concept of all mysticism, of whichever type."

According to LeShan, another common viewpoint of psychics and mystics is in the way they conceptualize time. Both view it as an illusion. There are not the discreet separations between past, present and future:

"Time," says the mystic, *"is a seamless garment in which man customarily makes arbitrary seams and separation lines."*

The statement of Jesus, "Before Abraham was, I am," expresses this even more clearly. Interestingly, LeShan goes on to discuss how the worldview of modern physicists also has much in common with that of the psychic and the mystic. The classical physicist sees the world of discreet objects and material points, whereas the modern physicist conceives of physical reality as represented by continuous fields and functions. Like the mystic who sees the world as impermanent and always changing, the physicists' new view of physical reality is that of activity and process with all things in a state of flux in relationship to the whole. Einstein said he arrived at his theory of relativity because he was so strongly convinced of the harmony of the universe. Heisenberg, in his ground breaking experiments with wave and particle behavior, demonstrated the "observer effect" in which the physicist himself influences and affects his observation to such a degree that he cannot separate his observation from himself. The results are a function of an interaction between oneself and reality.

Of course, these three groups – psychics, mystics and physicists – are completely different in their training, their goals and their tools and methods. Yet they arrive at similar views of reality. The goal of the mystic in meditation is to experience the Oneness behind the multiplicity of thoughts and sense perceptions. The goal of the modern physicist is to better understand the fundamental nature of reality that is behind the great diversity. Physicists today talk quantum theory, parallel universes, string theory and other esoteric ideas as they strive to find the Unified Theory of Everything. When the medium communicates with the spirit of a loved one who has passed, the essence of the experience is that in death there is no separation. Death of the physical body occurs but the spirit never dies and is with us always.

Thus, reality has many levels. Like a grove of aspen trees, to the observer each tree appears separate and independent of the others. However, at a deeper level they are one organism, all emanating from one root system. *"Oneness"* exists.

Often when one lets go of trying to arrive at an answer through their rational left-brain, inexplicably an insight may emerge. There is an in-flowing of awareness and sense of being connected to a greater whole.

Musicians like Mozart, Brahms and Aaron Copeland describe moments of creative breakthrough in which whole symphonies came to them in a flash of inspiration. Likewise, Einstein said his theory of relativity suddenly came to him as he idled time away in a canoe. Darwin reported that after years of collecting data the key elements of evolution fell into place in an instant while away from the workplace.

On a less profound level, I have had times when I've been busy trying to write something and working hard to find the right words, and then I've set it aside for a while. While doing something else, taking a shower or drying my hair – suddenly the perfect word or phrase "pops" into my head. In all these examples, when one sets aside the logical, rational left-brain thinking, a flash of insight suddenly emerges from this deeper whole. A level of reality where all is One.

Part IV.
My Journey To Oneness

"If you put your hands on this oar with me,
they will never harm another,
and they will come to find
they hold everything you want.

If you put your soul against this oar with me,
the power that made the universe will enter your sinew
from a source not outside your limbs
but from a holy realm that lives in us.

Exuberant is existence, time a husk.
When the moment cracks open,
ecstasy leaps out and devours space;
love goes mad with the blessings, like my words give.

Why lay yourself on the torturer's rack of the past and future?
The mind that tries to shape tomorrow beyond its capacities will find no rest.
Be kind to yourself, dear – to our innocent follies
Forget any sounds or touch you knew that did not help you dance.
You will come to see that all evolves us.

If you put your heart against the earth with me,
in serving every creature,
our beloved will enter you from our sacred realm
and we will be,
we will be so happy."
Rumi
A Year with Rumi: Daily Readings

The Search

*"Faith is the bird that feels the light
And sings when the dawn is still dark."*

Rabindranath Tagore
Fireflies

After meeting with the mediums, I was a woman on a mission. I felt a compelling need, almost an urgency to discover what had become of my husband. I was concerned that I might have only a window of time to find him before he slipped away entirely. Life took on a searching quality. I felt like something was pulling me. It was like some deeper truth or understanding was just around the corner and about to reveal itself

As I approached adulthood, I struggled to make sense of what happens to us after we die. I found it confusing - how does one know what to believe? Most of the world's religions go to great lengths to proclaim themselves as, not only different from, but also better than, all the others. Each religion seems to claim that their belief system is the only *right way* to believe and the others are wrong. How can that be? Are the millions of people in the world who don't believe in a particular way of thinking really going to hell?

As a child, I grew up having to attend the Lutheran Church and Sunday School. My mother was a Lutheran and took what was written in the Bible to be literally true. My father, on the other hand, said he was an atheist or an agnostic. When I asked him, "What do you believe?" he said, "I believe in the Golden Rule. We should treat others like we want to be treated." He rarely went to church with us. And on those infrequent occasions when my mother was able to persuade him to join us, he'd embarrass her by reading his pocket novel during the service. Everyone was happier when he didn't go.

After Daddy dropped us off in front of the church, Mamma, Sally and I walked down the long center aisle passing what seemed like hundreds of rows of long benches. She liked to sit near the front where she wouldn't miss a word the minister had to say. Looking down upon us in the sanctuary was a huge cross with Jesus' body hanging on it. The sad expression on his face and the blood dripping from his hands and feet where they put nails through him and tied him onto the cross made me want to cry. We had to sit on those hard benches for what seemed like an eternity. Sally and I began to fuss and squirm and kick the seats in front of us. When we talked out loud while everyone else was praying with their eyes closed, their heads bowed down, and hands folded, Mamma would scold us and get out the coloring books.

I found the minister in his long black robes scary. While he preached his sermon, his voice got louder and louder. He'd wave his arms in the air and then an angry look would come over his face. Sometimes he said things that frightened me, such as that every child comes into this world a sinner. This meant that I had done something really bad when I was just a tiny baby or even before I was born. But what that was, I had no idea. He said that the way we could save ourselves from going to hell when we die was to believe in Jesus Christ and take him to be our personal savior. But I found it hard to believe what the minister was saying about Jesus - that a long time ago some bad people captured Jesus and beat him and treated him terribly and then hung him on a cross to die. Then they put him in a cave and rolled a gigantic rock in front of it. But in the middle of the night Jesus came to life again and rolled the big stone away and rose up to heaven to be with God. I didn't see how that was possible. How could he come to life once he was dead? How did he rise up? Did his body float up into the sky? I didn't get it. This must mean I didn't believe in Jesus.

I didn't see how other Bible stories could be true either – like Noah's ark. God told Noah he was going to send a huge flood to destroy the world, and he asked Noah to build a big boat and save all the animals. So Noah was able to find a mommy and a daddy of every animal on the earth and get them all to behave themselves and walk in a straight line up onto the boat so that when the flood came they'd all be safe. My questioning mind could not grasp this. How could Noah find all the animals? And how could they all fit on his boat? How would he have enough food to feed them the whole time the boat was floating on the water? And what would he do with their poop?

To make matters worse, when I looked around the huge church, it seemed that the hundreds of people, mostly all grown-ups, seemed to believe what he was saying. Something was clearly wrong with *me*. It did confirm what the minister had said, that there was something bad, or sinful, about me. And, of course, this meant that when I died, I was a goner. I would go straight to hell. And that was too gruesome to think about. I was so relieved when the ordeal of church was over and Daddy came back to pick us up.

For many years after I left home, I didn't set foot in a church again unless it was to go to a wedding or some other ceremonial occasion. I'd had my fill of organized religion. But one day in graduate school I ventured into a Unitarian Universalist service. They spoke of the divine in each person, which I took to mean that at their core people are basically good. I liked that idea. When I look into the eyes of my grandchildren, it's easy for me to imagine a natural luminosity glowing from within. I'd always recoiled at the thought of a baby starting off from birth as being basically sinful, as if we arrive in the world already tainted.

I also liked that this church encouraged people to doubt and ask questions and to figure out for themselves what makes sense. They didn't tell people what to believe. There is no one "right" answer in the Unitarian church. They speak of Jesus and Moses, Mohammed and the Buddha and other great teachers in history who have made a difference to the world. What a contrast to the church of my childhood! I had finally found a spiritual home that could allow my curious mind to venture out and explore whatever grabbed my fancy.

And venture out I did. I couldn't believe that Ted had gone to be with the God in the heaven spoken of in my childhood Sunday School class, the heaven of flowers and butterflies, harps playing and angels flying around. Likewise, I couldn't believe in God as a white-bearded old man sitting on a throne in the sky, passing judgment on us down on earth. And yet on the other hand, I couldn't, or didn't want to believe that Ted's spirit, his essence, just stopped existing with the passing of his body. I continued to search for answers.

The Clear Light

My synchronistic encounter with the Buddhist therapist on Southwest Airlines gave direction to my search (see chapter, *An Encounter with Grace on Southwest Airlines*). It launched me on my journey into Buddhism and the Eastern religions. This new friend had spoken about *The Tibetan Book of Living and Dying*, in which Sogyal Rinpoche writes about oneness, death and reincarnation. I got off the plane and headed for the nearest bookstore, hot on the trail of finding out what had become of my husband. I was excited. Since the beginning of time, I thought, people have been intrigued by these questions, like what happens to us after we die. I wondered what wisdom I might find in the words of the masters. As I scanned the Buddhism section at the bookstore, my eyes came to rest on Sogyal's book. My heart skipped a beat.

Later, and to my great surprise, I also learned that in Lexington, Massachusetts, the very town where I live, there was a Tibetan Buddhist group who were followers of Sogyal Rinpoche. They met every week to listen to a dharma talk (like a sermon), meditate and socialize. I felt I was onto something. This had to be auspicious, as the Buddhists like to say. I might not only find out where Ted is, I thought with a smile, but I might meet a new, wonderful Buddhist-type man who is still in the flesh. I might kill two birds with one stone so to speak, or maybe I should say, resurrect two wonderful men in one fell swoop.

Sogyal Rinpoche wrote about the *bardos,* which are the stages a soul passes through after death and before it is reborn, or reincarnated. These teachings have been traced back to ancient times and handed down by Padmasambhava, who introduced Buddhism to Tibet.

The bardo that is seen at the moment of death is referred to as *Clear Light or Ground Luminosity*. According to the teachings, the dying person experiences a luminous, clear light that represents their innermost essence and as the fundamental nature of everything. When I thought of the double rainbow that stretched out across the river where Ted had died, I was elated. It seemed to me that if Ted had experienced the Clear Light upon his death, perhaps his way of letting me know about this stunning phenomenon was to send rainbows. When Ted was living, he had often wondered what it is like to die. He lamented that even though his father had taught him many things, he had not been able to share any wisdom about death.

So Ted sent rainbows. He wanted to do for me what his father hadn't been able to do for him. When clear light is broken down into its elements, it casts a spectrum of many beautiful colors – like the crystals that hang in my kitchen window. When light shines through these prisms, they radiate beautiful rainbows all over the room.

During another bardo, an intensive life review takes place in which we are both the judge and the judged of our past life. The new family we are born into is the karmic result of our past actions in our previous life. I found it interesting to read that during this bardo, the dead soul has an awareness of life going on here on this earthly realm and can observe his loved ones still living.

I was intrigued to read that both Sogyal Rinpoche, and the Dalai Lama (see his book *Dzogchen)*, recognize many parallels between some of the features of the bardos and the near-death experience. The near-death experience has been reported throughout history by writers and philosophers as varied as Plato, Tolstoy and Jung, as well as countless ordinary people.

The thousands of reports of people who nearly died, or died and then were revived, bear a striking resemblance to each other. They contain some of the following features: an out of-body experience in which one views his body as from above; moving through a long, dark tunnel and being drawn almost magnetically toward a clear, bright light in the distance; approaching a loved one or a compassionate spiritual figure like God or Christ; witnessing a life review, and then reaching a boundary beyond which one cannot pass and being told to return to the body and this life. Sometimes, one is told to return with a mission to carry out.

The near-death experience is almost universally positive, often resulting in losing one's fear of death. As a result of surviving a NDE, the person is often transformed and returns to life more loving, tolerant and interested in spiritual values.

I have read many accounts of people who have had near-death experiences, but I was especially fascinated when a good friend of mine told me about what happened to her many years ago. When she was about 28 years old she became seriously ill, had to be hospitalized and underwent surgery. She was given general anesthesia and while her body was being operated on she had following experience:

"I was walking down this long hallway. At the end of it stood my father who had died many years earlier. He was standing there at the end of the hall with his arms open wide, like he was waiting for me, ready to bring me over to him. I saw a bright light behind him. I kept walking toward him. Just as I was getting close to him, I could feel myself move up and out of my body. I could look down and see myself. It was all very peaceful. And then the next thing I knew, I was conscious and awake in the recovery room. The surgery was over."

She went on to say:

"Because of the extraordinary experience I'd just had, I asked if anything had happened during the surgery. One of the nurses told me that at one point my blood pressure had dropped precipitously low. Ever since then I've had no fear of death. When my time comes, I will not be afraid to die."

The Dalai Lama and Sogyal Rinpoche have both said that the bright light in the near-death-experience may be a similar to the Clear Light bardo of death. Sogyal goes on to see other similarities in the stages experienced at death, including the out-of-body experience, meeting others who have died and the life review. Later, however, I was disappointed to learn that belief in the bardos is not common among Buddhists in general, only the Tibetan Buddhists.

The dead watch their relatives on the earthly plane grieve but are unable to communicate with them to let them know, "I'm fine up here, there is no reason to suffer." I thought of the readings I have had with mediums. The dead come through to let us know that they are still with us in spirit and that they are aware of what we are going through.

I find it thrilling when two very different, unrelated sources arrive at similar conclusions. They validate each other in my mind. They lead me to think that Ted's spirit continues in some way. Of course, I have no idea about what is really true. How can anyone know? What I do believe is that it is easier to be open to the mystery than to be skeptical and closed-minded. Being open to possibility gives me hope. And then amazing worlds of ideas can emerge. Over the years, what began as my quest to find Ted, or whatever became of his energy, morphed into an ever-expanding, ever-deepening exploration of Eastern philosophy and mysticism.

The Mystery

Along the way, as I continued to seek answers to what happens to us after we die, I read countless books about death and dying, psychic phenomena, mysticism, Eastern philosophy and religions. I have often wondered why I have been drawn toward all of these types of spiritual teachings that many Westerners feel are just hocus-pocus. Certainly part of my exploration was that I hoped I would find out what had become of my husband. But it's still puzzling. My other widow friends didn't seem to be on a similar quest to find answers to these big questions. And I'm sure they loved their husbands as much as I loved Ted.

But as I think about it now, they likely have been on their own journeys, seeking to find something helpful to cope with the deaths of their husbands, too. It's just that the nature of what each of us has found to be meaningful has differed from one another.

Nonetheless, at night I'd turn on the electric blanket, put my pajamas in the dryer to warm up (a little trick I learned in a bereavement group), make myself a cup of hot tea and crawl into my bed. There I'd open my book, eager to discover what new worlds were going to be revealed to me this evening. I reached for something larger than myself that would take me out of my own small, contracted life, and give me hope.

The teachings of the Eastern religions were like a balm that soothed the ache in my chest. They offered a light, a candle in the darkness that beckoned me. The words of Jelaluddin Rumi, a Sufi mystic in the 13th century (which are inscribed on his tomb stone) call out:

"Come, Come, whoever you are!
Wanderer, worshipper, lover or leaving,
Ours is not a caravan of despair, come.
Even if you've broken your vows a thousand times,
Come, and yet again
Come!"

In another of his poems he writes:

"Out beyond ideas of
Wrong-doing and right-doing
There is a field.
I'll meet you there
When the soul lies down in the grass
And the world is too full to talk about..."

Coleman Banks
The Illuminated Rumi

I imagined that out beyond what I could perceive, Ted's spirit was still with me. And although I could no longer see or hear him, I liked to believe that he could, in some way, see me. I often imagined that he was watching me – when I carried out the trash in the dark night, when I headed off alone on a three-hour car ride, when I sat down to do my taxes, when I worried if I had enough money to make it to the "end" – all the zillions of times when I felt so alone. And I liked to believe that out in that field, beyond our known material world, I would one day be with him again. I felt comforted and my mind felt opened and expanded, and I began to feel a connectedness to life in ways I'd never felt before. I wondered what drew ne toward finding comfort and inspiration in something beyond myself? Could that part of me come to my own rescue?

Perhaps it was the influence of my beloved grandparents who enlarged my world and planted the seeds of curiosity in me. Grama and Pags (as we called my grandfather because as little children we couldn't pronounce "grandpa") were the light of my life. When I think of the summers I spent with them at their ranch in the Colorado Rockies, a cascade of delicious memories fills my heart – lying in the hammock with Grama making up stories about fascinating creatures floating by in the fluffy white clouds; irrigating the meadows with Pags and his showing us gopher holes and tunnels and telling us about their underground lives; black currant picking with Grama at her "secret" spots in the high mountains.

I felt special standing on Pags' feet as we danced to his favorite song, "Beautiful Dreamer," playing on the old Victorola record player. I was entranced as I snuggled on Grama's lap as she read *The Wizard of Oz* and *Alice in Wonderland*. She told us about her life growing up on a farm in Kansas, and how scared she was of tornados after her mother had died. Grama often sang to us, "Poor little babes lost in the woods." Only later did I realize the meaning of this song to her when I learned of the frightening experiences she'd had of being lost in the tall cornfields.

Sometimes on a clear night, Pags took us out to look for the Big Dipper, the North Star and other constellations. At our ranch, which was miles away from the nearest town, the stars were so brilliant that they looked like a dazzling carpet of light overhead. Pags told us about how the Milky Way is like a gigantic spiral or wheel, and our little planet Earth is orbiting around on one rim of it, with the rest of the wheel stretching back farther than our minds can imagine.

When we drove to Breckenridge for our weekly shopping trip, Grama would often gaze up at the peaks towering above us and remark, "Can you believe that a

long time ago an ocean covered all these mountains?" We found actual evidence for this ancient ocean when we played on a shale hillside near the ranch. While Pags cleaned out the ditches dammed up by beavers, Grama, Sally, and I searched for snails and clam fossils. Sometimes, we also found little meteorites embedded in the shale

that Pags said came from the sky above. I loved hearing Grama tell the story of how my family's earliest pioneers traveled to Colorado by covered wagon and stagecoach in hopes of striking it rich and making a better life for themselves. She said my great grandparents had made the last part of the difficult journey up and over the 14,000' Continental Divide by horseback, each carrying a little baby in their arms. These and so many other stories told to me by my grandparents first stretched my imagination. They opened me to a life of wondering that continues to this day.

Discoveries

"A broken heart is a wide opened heart."
Unknown

And so, after Ted died, I was drawn toward wanting to learn more about what lay beyond my horizon. My exploration of the various beliefs took me down many random trails. I felt like one of my pioneer ancestors prospecting for gold as I followed a vein of glitter up one streambed, and then another and another, until ultimately one day coming upon the mother lode from which they all had come. Each spiritual trail was interesting in its own right as it branched out in various directions. But I was thrilled to discover that a single universal truth shines at the core of all major religions – and that is *love.*

Practicing compassion is the thread running through the teachings of Confucius, Moses, Muhammad, the Buddha and, of course, Jesus, who preached, "Love your enemies as yourself." They all teach us to look into our own hearts, discover what gives us pain and then refuse, under any circumstances, to inflict that pain on anyone.

I also found it fascinating to learn that all the liberal branches of the world religions, including Christian mysticism, Advaita Vedanta in Hinduism, Kabbalah in Judaism, Sufism of the Islamic religion, and Dzogchen in Buddhism, share similar conceptions of the nature of reality. The words they use are different, but there is much commonality and overlap in their central ideas.

These ideas expanded my view of reality. They helped me to believe that more exists than what we see. They speak of two different dimensions, the world of *Form* and the world of the *Formless.* The world of *Form* is everything we can perceive with our five senses and take in with our amazing, but limited, brain. It is my house with all its "stuff," my bed, the vase of flowers, my teacup, my friends, my family, the sun the moon the stars. It is also my thoughts – both profound and mundane – and my feelings of sadness, my loneliness, my joy, my anger and so forth.

Everything in the world of *Form* is impermanent. Nothing lasts. Everything arises, exists for a while and then disappears. That's the bad news and the good news. Good times don't last, but neither do the bad. Sadness comes, sadness goes. My understanding of impermanence helped get me through many a dark night when life seemed futile. I came to realize that even in the worst of times, when I thought surely my heart could not withstand this amount of pain, the next day I'd awaken in quite a different place. The sun would be shining again. The world looked fresh and hope had returned. Now you might say, "Death seems pretty permanent to me; you can't change that." And that's true, of course, but even when the situation is intractable, as if it's written in stone, one's *response* to it can change its devastating impact.

Buddhism teaches that suffering is caused when we become attached to something that is impermanent. We fiercely hold onto that which will not last. Children grow up and leave, loved ones die, beauty fades and old age creeps up on us. We may become overly protective and grasp onto our children, apply creams and facelifts to our wrinkles, exercise frenetically at the gym, but ultimately we're going to fail.

Some, of course, will say, "Then what's the point of loving someone, if they're only going to leave us or die one day?" The secret is to be able to more fully live in the moment, appreciating the preciousness of what is happening right here and right now, knowing this will not last forever. And then, when the time comes, being able to let it go. That is the challenge.

Then there is another dimension, *The Formless* - the Mystery out of which all forms are born and into which all forms dissolve. This transcendent realm is sometimes called God, Allah, Higher Power, the Source, Spirit, the Mystery, even the Force (as in *Star Wars*' *"May the Force be with you"*). Hinduism calls it *Brahman*, the *Ground of Being* that gives rise to all life. Although Buddhists don't believe in a Supreme Being as such, they have often likened these two dimensions to the waves and the ocean. From the silent depths of the ocean, the individual waves arise, exist for a while, and then dissolve back into the ocean.

In *Conversations with God*, Neal Donald Walsh writes about the process of the transcendent becoming imminent, or how the Formless – the spiritual world – permeates the world of Form:

> *"Because that which is Divine yearns to experience itself, to know itself completely, experientially, it enters the realm of the Relative in individuated Form. Divine Spirit emerges from the All ... through an endless multitude of distinctive expressions."*

It is like God putting on clothes. Another way of describing this phenomenon is that if you shine a flashlight out into the sky, you cannot see the beam of light. The light has to be shined onto something, some material object, in order to see it. God, or the Source, is invisible – it takes the world of Form to sense its presence.

These ideas appealed to me because I liked thinking that a spark of the divine exists in every being, rather than thinking of God existing as an entity "out there" somewhere.

According to the Big Bang theory – which is the most widely accepted explanation for how the universe came into being – nearly 14 billion years ago all the matter in the cosmos existed in a form smaller than a subatomic particle. From this singularity, an enormous explosion and rapid expansion occurred leading to the formation of all the galaxies and the entire world of Form that we know today.

The universe has not evolved in a random, chaotic and haphazard way. Scientists have shown that there are patterns and cycles and a direction to the unfolding of the universe. Over the billions of years there has been an ever increasing complexity of life.

The amazing diversity of our world boggles my mind. When I take a walk outside and notice, I mean really notice, the world around me, I am deeply moved. I especially enjoy the springtime. The infinite array of colors, shapes and textures of the foliage coming to life after winter's severity is a feast for my eyes. The enormous variety of flowers, each blossom which is so exquisitely lovely – it's as if each has been created by some master craftsman. It's like opening a door to the sacred. A deeper part of myself resonates with the sheer beauty of it all. It nourishes the soul. All this cannot be random; it seems to me that there has to be a greater intelligence underlying and permeating our existence.

The various spiritual traditions have given many names to this spark of the divine that dwells within and animates all living beings. Christians call it Christ within, Buddhists call it Buddha nature or Indwelling Perfection; the Quakers speak of greeting "That of God in every person;" the Kabbalists think of each person as a shard of the exploded God. Hindus call it Atman and say that at the core of everything stirs the hidden pulse of Brahman. Others may call it the Soul, Consciousness, Essence, The Witness or The Self.

That part of myself that feels deeply touched when I experience the grandeur of nature – the majesty of towering mountain peaks, the serenity of a tranquil lake, the towering redwoods, the vastness of the night-time sky, the mystery of a caterpillar's transformation from worm to a butterfly – is my own essential self, the divine within myself.

Likewise, when we experience the inherent goodness and the divine within others, we are put in touch with our own divine nature. I was brought to tears when I heard about a little girl who was paralyzed for life by a gunman's stray bullet and how, from her wheelchair, she spoke to the gunman and told him she wasn't mad at him. Similarly, I was deeply moved when I heard about a young Asian man who lost his wife and two young children when an airplane crashed into his house. He spoke to the pilot, who had ejected safely, and said he hoped he would be able to let go of any guilt he carried and forgive himself.

I had a clear sense of the dimension of this indwelling spirit when I went with Scott to view Ted's body in the mortuary. As I looked at that inert body lying in the casket, what hit me most profoundly was the stark reality that my husband was gone. It was definitely his body, but that essence, that energy that made him who he was, was no longer there.

Since we all come from the same Source, and that same innermost Essence that pulsates in me energizes all living creatures, we are all One. However, on another level, our personality and ego differentiate us from each other and we may feel separate and alone. Yet on the deepest level we are all connected. Furthermore, we all have the desire to be treated with dignity, to feel joy and to love and be loved.

Although I had lost my dear husband, something remarkable had happened to me along the way. My quest had taken me out of my small, contracted, lonely view of the world to feeling expanded and deepened. I felt connected to all of life.

I realize that some of these words – Essence, Interconnectedness, Oneness, Compassion – can just sound like dry, intellectual concepts, so let me give you an example of how these teachings provide depth and meaning to my life. In the early days of my grief I wrote the following excerpt in my journal:

Gift From A Blind Woman

I am having one of those bad days, one of those days when I long for Ted so acutely that everything seems pointless. Bleak. I cannot bear to go back to my lifeless house where emptiness hits me in the face when I step inside the door.

So I take myself to Starbucks, to humanity. I find a seat by the window and insert myself into the bustle of life: people coming, people going; lovers meeting; friends happy in greeting; others engrossed in reading. The faint odor of coffee and rich pastries filters through my consciousness arousing distant memories of home, caring for and being cared for. The warm cappuccino slides down my throat and soothes the ache in my chest. Clinking of spoons on coffee cups, clattering of dishes, hissing and sputtering of the espresso maker against a background hum of voices. A balm for my shredded heart; I feel connected to life.

I glance out the window. The drab, slate-gray sky reflects my desolate mood. A solitary raven holds vigil on a high wire, waiting. My eye settles on a lone figure sitting on a bench, a blind woman. My attention awakens and is drawn to her. Sitting at her feet is a golden retriever guide dog, loyal, attentive, and quietly protective. An aura of devotedness and strength about him gives me the feeling that he would gladly-in-an-instant lay down his life to protect his special woman.

I feel strangely bonded to her. As I watch, a man comes along, someone she seems to know. They sit together, share a bit of food from a bag he was carrying and after a little while he moves on. I'm struck by the very ordinariness of the event, a man and a woman coming together, a sharing and then a moving apart. And yet in the midst of this commonplace experience, something profound speaks to me. The woman, the dog, the man put me in touch with kindness, with compassion and strength. I feel her courage to live in the face of what must be tremendous obstacles and challenges. I feel humbled by her. I am taken out of my self-absorbed suffering and I realize that many people live their lives with a disability or some other intractable situation. And they do it so gracefully. All I have to do is open my eyes and look beyond my own pain. I can find myself in others, and so, be healed.

I didn't just feel a connectedness to her. I felt a Oneness with her. *I am her,* I thought. *I am her isolation and her fear. And I am her courage as she faces darkness and the unknown. I am her appreciation of friendship, loyalty and kindness.*

I look around me and realize that I can find myself everywhere. I am the little child across the coffee shop kicking the table legs, beginning to fuss, unhappy and restless. I am the mother feeling a rising frustration, but trying to hold it together and be patient. I am the teenager in the midst of the group, clothed in black and decorated with piercings, feeling awkward and trying to fit in; I am those young lovers oblivious to the world around them, smitten by love; I am all these people.

I am grateful to the blind woman. She threw me a lifeline that day. She took me out of my self-absorbed suffering and helped me feel not so alone. Indeed, I'm grateful for this entire journey. It opened me to life as I had not known it before.

Interconnectedness – Ripples Over Time

"O hidden life, vibrant in every atom,
O hidden light, shining in every creature,
O hidden love, embracing all in oneness,
May all who feel themselves as one with thee
Know they are therefore one with every other."

Unknown

A core tenant of Buddhist philosophy is that of emptiness and impermanence, which says: we don't exist as a separate entity with a fixed core because everything about us is transitory. Our feelings change from moment to moment, our thoughts come and go, and certainly, our bodies change. All the cells in our bodies have been replaced many times over the course of our lifetime.

I was not entirely comfortable with this idea. It felt so insubstantial. I said to myself, *I feel like I am something. So what am I?*

One day I attended a workshop with Robert Thurman, a renowned scholar of Tibetan Buddhism, and came away with some new insights. Thurman teaches that we are *relational beings*: every part of us has come about as a result of relating to the outside world. We are connected to and are a part of the world around us in every aspect of our being. Every breath we take comes from the air around us; every thought we've ever had, every emotion we've ever felt originates from an interaction with the external world. Our skin holds us together and makes us look like separate beings, but we have permeable boundaries. We are little bodies of interacting energy fields walking around influencing each other and being influenced by others. Nothing lives in a vacuum.

To give an example, one Thanksgiving, my six-year-old grandson and I baked a loaf of pumpkin bread for the family dinner. As I had him dump the sugar in the mixing bowl and showed him how to measure a teaspoon of soda and level it off with the edge of a knife, I recalled Grama showing me how to measure and sift and spoon and stir as we baked her famous Christmas sugar cookies. I was that child again feeling her warm, loving presence. And now I can also know, being a grandmother myself, that rich feeling she must have had teaching us, her little grandchildren, how to bake. I also can see these invisible lines of connection projecting into the future. One day my grandson will be showing his child, or grandchild, how to make something. I imagine all these lines of connection extending for generations back into the past and radiating infinitely forward into the future – like the map I found in the American Airlines booklet that shows all the lines that fan out from all the connecting cities it flies to across the United States and the world. And that's just one layer! I think of all the many other layers of connection that goes into the making of the pumpkin bread – someone grew the pumpkin, picked it, hauled it off to market, processed and canned it, and loaded it onto truck and the chain continued until one day I bought the can off the shelf at the market. And then there's the eggs, someone raised the hens that laid the eggs, and so forth and so on…That's just pulling on a couple strands in this amazing tapestry we call life. Layer upon layer of woven together connections that are over-lapping, re-combining, and unfolding over time.

A more poignant example of the interconnectedness of life, also involving my grandmother, comes to mind. I have always felt terribly guilty about the fact that I didn't go out to Colorado to her funeral. I was 31 years old when she died – hardly a child – but I have no memory of visiting her when she was dying or going to her funeral. I did have four children at that time, the youngest being only four months old, but I dearly loved my grandmother and there's no reason why Ted couldn't have taken care of them for a couple of days. How could I have been so self-centered, so heartless?

And then one day I was looking through some books in my grandmother's antique desk and came across the old Peabody family Bible. Tucked away inside it was a torn open envelope with my grandmother's handwriting on the outside stating, *"To be opened upon my death."* (signed) *Victoria R. Peabody."* Inside were two pieces of paper. On the first she had written out a few words that could be used for her obituary. She stated just the bare essentials – when and where she was born, where she was educated, and when she married. She mentioned that one son (my father) *"was born of this union"* and the date when my grandfather died. That was it.

On the other sheet of paper were a few terse lines indicating what she wanted to happen with her body and the funeral service.

"I wish the following could be carried out – cremate –
When death occurs, have my body taken by the most convenient mortuary.
Please put pajamas on the body
Rent a coffin – I prefer a slab.
Omit all prayers, singing, flowers and services.
Have the ashes taken to Crown Hill and put besides Clif
Make the notice in paper as <u>short</u> as possible
Do not notify friends nor family.
I wish for privacy and quietness at funeral rites
I do not fear death –"

Victoria R. Peabody

Discovering these letters from my grandmother shed a whole new light on my sense of having betrayed her. Now I can see why I didn't go to her funeral – my father, in respecting her wishes, may not have even told me she had died. (At this point I can't remember if I was told or not.) But even if he had, he would have instructed me not to come out. There would be no funeral.

In writing out her wishes, Grama may not have realized that she was also depriving us, her family who loved her, the opportunity to grieve, to remember her and to celebrate her life and all she had meant to us. Funerals are for the living.

It seemed clear that Grama wanted the whole affair to be carried out as expeditiously as possible – like putting out the trash. *"Just put my body on a slab, dress it in pajamas – whatever is easiest – don't have a service of any sort and do not notify friends nor family."* It's as if she felt no one would care that she had died. It breaks my heart reading her words and thinking about how unloved and worthless she still felt in her last days. In spite of having had an uncommonly loving relationship with my grandfather and all the happy times spent with our family through the years, she still felt like that motherless child who had been so wounded decades earlier.

I learned about my grandmother's unhappy childhood growing up in Kansas by discovering another letter she had written to my father at a critical time in his life. Although she was a private woman, she felt compelled to explain to him why she had pushed him so hard in school:

> *"...We got little or no attention. My mother was always sick. I never remember the time when she wasn't. She died when I was about ten a little past. And in all my life, Clifton, I can never recall my mother ever holding me in her arms or on her lap, kissing me, or loving me. I have no memory of any one ever caressing me, Ida, Annie, Lottie or none of them. When I think of the forlorn little piece of humanity that I was trundling to school, undernourished, probably dirty, and poorly clad, fighting for myself like a little wild cat, trying to learn."*

She goes on to say how important becoming a teacher was to her. She managed to get herself to Colorado, where she taught in a one-room schoolhouse in Roggen:

> *"I had to live above the railroad station, do all my own janitor work, cook, got head lice. If there had been any one in the world to care they never would have let me stay there over night, but the $50 a month salary meant Greeley for me. I was just determined I was going to be something in the world. I got my Bachelor's degree in June, 1908. Not one member of my family was present, no one praised me, not a gift, not a thing the most of this time."*

Now you need to understand that my grandmother was not a complaining person. This is the only account of her early childhood I have ever heard. And yet I find it fascinating that so much of who she was as a person was passed down for better and for worse. I have her stoicism – it took me years of therapy to allow anyone to see my tears – and I have her determination, her resilience as well as her love of learning. My first book, "Horse 'n Buggy through Colorado" was really a 9th grade, joint-undertaking with Grama. She, of course, is a vital part of the writing of this book. In reading her account of how no one ever held or caressed her, I can also appreciate how much pleasure she got out of holding me on her lap and rubbing my back when I was a child.

Because Grama kept these painful early experiences locked inside her all her life, she carried these wounds to the grave. But, as it turns out she didn't protect anyone from their deleterious effects. Because I hadn't read these accounts of her own difficult growing up experiences and also her wishes about what she wanted to have happen after her death, I was left with such guilt at not having been a more loving granddaughter.

If Grama had the benefits of psychotherapy or had shared her early painful experiences with a good friend, she could have come to realize she was not unlovable and worthless just because she'd never been truly loved as a child.

These were just a couple of examples related to my grandmother that demonstrate how we influence and are influenced by others. I think of the myriad of ways Ted and I became intertwined over the years. Many of his expressions and mannerisms became mine and my ways became his. After 35 years we'd become so intricately woven together it is now impossible for me to pick out what I'd absorbed from him and what was my own unique way of being, independent from who he was. Of course there is nothing really original with anyone – every thought, feeling or "new" idea we've ever had comes from an interaction with the external world – yet we do have our unique ways that, when put together, express all of what we take in from the outside world.

Oneness and Compassion

"We're all bozos on the bus,
So we might as well sit back
And enjoy the ride."

Wavy Gravy

Sometimes when I'm in some public gathering place – like at a busy intersection in downtown Boston, or at a shopping mall, or waiting for my plane at the airport – I stop whatever is preoccupying my mind and I drop into the moment. And I just *notice*.

The other day, I was in Harvard Square sitting outside, enjoying an ice cream and watching the people go by. Such a cross-section of humanity! I saw a mother pushing her infant in a buggy, a young couple in love strolling arm in arm, a frail old man limping along with a cane, two little girls skipping happily hand in hand, a woman in running shorts striding vigorously on her power walk, a homeless man pushing a grocery buggy piled high with all his worldly belongings scavenged from local dumpsters. I was struck by all the countless forms of life streaming by.

When we focus on these surface differences, we can tend to look at others through judgmental eyes. We can set ourselves apart from others by sticking a label on them in our mind. He/she is, *A nerd... not the brightest bulb on the tree...filthy rich...dressed like a hooker... young and naïve... old and decrepit...a penny pincher...a bean pole.* We elevate ourselves in our minds (or we might devalue ourselves if we label ourselves in these terms). When we look at people through the lens of our personality we separate ourselves from others.

But as I sat there in Harvard Square, I suddenly became deeply moved watching this flow of humanity. I felt an expansion come over me. My mind moved beyond my own limited self-preoccupation and opened to the world around me. A wave of tenderness rose up in my chest, tenderness for all of us, my fellow travelers. I thought: 'We are all like bubbles trying to navigate our way, floating, bumping down the stream of life. Each of us is on our unique journey, and yet it is the same journey. Some of us are at the beginning of our trip and others are nearing the end. Sometimes the current is rough and treacherous and we get knocked around, and at other times it is smooth sailing and we linger in calm waters. We all just want to find a little joy! We all are faced with hard stuff.

I remember a little sign I once saw thumb tacked to someone's wall:

"Be Kind.
Remember...
Everyone you meet is fighting a hard battle."

To look at most people, they appear on the surface to be going about their business. But one never knows what is going on inside another person, what demons they're struggling with, what keeps them awake at night. Instead of reacting critically to other persons whose behavior is annoying, I can open my eyes to the suffering, and to the courage, underneath.

When I am able to see beyond the surface appearance of another person, I can connect with the essence of that person – and on that deeper level there is no difference. We all have experienced the full range of human feelings, to one degree or another, at one time or another. Like the bubbles on the water, we all come from the same source and we all return to the same source. The same energy or spirit that animates one of us animates us all. Or in Eckart Tolle's words:

"Everything is not only connected with everything else, but also with the source of life out of which it came."

The Dalai Lama once said:

"If you want to be happy, practice compassion. If you want others to be happy, practice compassion."

I find this to be the secret that works almost every time when I am feeling lonely or sad. All I have to do is pick up the phone and reach out in kindness to someone else who might be going through hard stuff. I always feel much better. It is a gift I discovered I can give to myself. I never have to feel alone again. Although at 3 am, when those heart-wrenching fears arise in my busy mind, my friend may not appreciate hearing my voice on the phone saying, "Hi – I was thinking about you and wondering how you're doing." I may have to hold on until the morning to make myself feel better.

Enjoying my ice cream in the warm sunshine on the bench that day in Cambridge, my eye was drawn to a young boy sitting by himself on another bench bouncing a small rubber ball. He must have been about 13 years old, a shy, skinny kid dressed in clothing I'm sure his peers would've called very un-cool. Over and over he bounced and caught the ball. Occasionally between bounces he glanced sideways out of his eyes at a group of three or four teenagers hanging out not far away. He seemed to know them. They were definitely cool. Longish hair, baggy T-shirts underneath hooded sweatshirts, and low-slung pants that seemed to barely hang onto their non-existent hips. They were having a good time and clearly were comfortable with each other as they laughed, joked and jostled one another. The lone boy continued to bounce his ball, over and over. After a while he pulled out his iPhone, and put on some headphones. I didn't know if he was making a call or just entertaining himself.

Then he got up and walked away. Suddenly my memory flashed back to my own junior high school days. I have been that left-out kid wanting so desperately to fit in.

My heart went out to that young boy bouncing his ball, not knowing how to navigate the distance between him and the other kids. Who hasn't felt that exquisite pain of feeling apart from others?

I've also been on the other side. I've been in a group of friends, caught up in conversation and probably oblivious to someone sitting on the periphery who might have liked to have been included. Or worse still, I know there have been times when I've been aware of someone on the outside and I did not invite her to join us. I've been all of these people. I can feel compassion, not only for the person feeling excluded, but for the persons doing the excluding.

Eckert Tolle's words come to mind:

"To love is to recognize yourself in another person."

Sympathetic Joy

One weekend, my good friend and her husband invited me to join them at their summer vacation home. After dinner we sat chatting in the living room. During our conversation, I was aware of his rubbing her feet as she curled up next to him on the sofa. The amazing thing for me was that I enjoyed it, too. I did not pine for Ted. I did not hate them for having what I had lost. Instead, I could take pleasure in their happiness and the comfort they felt with each other. They gave me the opportunity to re-experience those delicious times when my husband had rubbed my feet and we were so comfortable in our familiarity.

I have a similar experience when I observe a mother holding a small child who snuggles on her lap. As I watch them, I am once again holding my own child or grandchild and feeling those delicious sensations of the weight of a baby nestled in my arms, the warmth of her skin on my skin, the soft, powdery baby smell of her hair. I am also the little child. Sweet memories come to me of snuggling in my own grandmother's lap, feeling happy and content with her strong arms surrounding me. I feel at one with the woman and with her child. Buddhism calls it *Sympathetic Joy*, that attitude of rejoicing in the happiness and good fortune of others. It is one of Buddhism's *Four Immeasurables*, along with *Love, Compassion* and *Equanimity*. I have discovered, having come to the other side of grief, that I am able to feel a sense of oneness with, not only the suffering of others, but with their joy as well.

I especially enjoy watching couples; couples at church; couples on the subway; couples at parties; couples anywhere. I notice, and most often, can enjoy seeing couples exchange those easy familiarities – his arm around her, her hand resting lightly on his thigh, the knowing glances that pass between their eyes, the whispered exchanges.

I am reminded of a time when I went for lunch at a local restaurant that I frequent when I have free time between appointments. On this particular day, after buying my favorite salad and a cup of cappuccino, I settled into a booth with my book and writing materials. After a few moments, I noticed an older couple, probably in their 60s or 70s sitting at the next table. They were not at all physically striking in any kind of way, but something about them drew my attention. I noticed a kind of softness between them. I could see and hear the man better because the woman had her back to me. The tone of his voice struck me – so soft and gentle. There was kindness in his eyes and warmth in his voice as he spoke to her. Occasionally their fingers reached out and touched each other across the table. I reveled in it.

In my early days of grieving I would have felt a rush of sadness and missing Ted. I would have felt envious that they had what I had lost. It wasn't that long ago when, if I'd see a frail older man helping his even-more frail wife cross the street, a wave of resentment would ripple through me. Why didn't Ted and I have the chance to be frail old people together, helping each other navigate the precarious last stages of life! Why do I have to go it alone?

But these days, witnessing the tenderness between others puts me in touch with the tenderness and love inside myself. I can recall the many times when I had experienced this with Ted. Witnessing love between another couple allows me to enjoy love again. Just because Ted is no longer here *physically* doesn't mean my experience of tenderness is gone. It will never leave me. I felt grateful to this older couple sitting next to me for putting me in touch with those intimate feelings within myself. I was happy for them, *and* happy for *myself*.

The Oneness of Pain and Joy

It is strange how grief has a way of ambushing us. I remember one 4th of July several years after Ted died. I had thought my grief was long gone. But as I noticed family groups that afternoon, carrying their picnic baskets and streaming into the carnival fair grounds, I slipped into a nostalgic mood. My mind circled back to that last 4th of July my husband and I celebrated together – just ten days before the end of his life.

To celebrate our nation's birthday, Ted and I had gone to Boston with a couple of friends where we picnicked on the esplanade, listened to the magnificent music of the Boston Pops orchestra, and were awed by a dazzling display of fireworks in the clear night-time sky. We were thrilled as explosions of sound and lights erupted overhead, culminating in one dramatic spectacle of brilliance.

And then – abruptly – it was over. The splendor we'd witnessed fell into silence and was swallowed by darkness. Little did we know this was soon to be our fate as well.

On another 4th of July evening many years later, I had dinner with a widow friend of mine. Since the night was still young, we went to her home to watch the video *Moonstruck*. We must have been in a masochistic mood. I was not prepared for its impact. My life had gone in such a different direction over the last several years – grandchildren, work, and activities with friends – I had forgotten that romance still existed in this world. Scenes from the movie brought it all back – with a vengeance. Watching Cher fall in love with the tall, handsome man brought me to my knees. Once again, I remembered that delicious feeling of running my hands across the ripples of Ted's broad shoulders and that tender feeling of his reaching out and holding my hand so gently in his big hand, and of hugging him and kissing him and holding him and feeling his arms around me and never, ever wanting to let him go. I drove home in tears. It had been months since I'd felt this longing. The pain still cut through me like a knife.

I suppose that from time to time, the loneliness that comes from longing for Ted and missing him will rear its ugly, beautiful head. Actually, I wouldn't want it any other way. The pain only hurts so terribly because it opens me up to those deep memories of what I treasured. What I had with Ted will always be with me.

Pain and love walk hand in hand. Life is a flow from light to dark and dark to light – from joy to pain, from pain to joy. I've learned the trick is to go with the flow and not think of joy and pain as good or bad. Darkness and light are not opposites as I had usually thought of them, but a part of a greater whole. They are part of the mystery that both hides and reveals itself. In the midst of the worst of times there is a light that, if I am open to it, will reveal itself. When I see happily in-love couples on the screen or hear Celine Dion singing the *Power of Love* and feel the sharp pangs of yearning rise up in my heart, I am then able to pull up those rich delicious memories of being with Ted. I linger once again in the warmth of his arms and the softness of his eyes.

Likewise, the shadow of darkness was hidden in some of my happiest moments with Ted. I remember many a night as we snuggled together in our favorite spoon position, saying to each other, "Ah, the best part of the day." But even as we drifted off to sleep, happy and content, sometimes Ted would remind me of the hard reality that this would not last forever. The day would eventually come when one of us would go on alone. Around some corner death laid waiting – we just didn't know which one. I think it helped us to appreciate the precious moments we had together and to soak them up.

This brings to mind an experience I had walking the labyrinth. A labyrinth is a maze-like design originating in ancient Greek times and is often used these days as a form of walking meditation. As I walked the labyrinth's circuitous route towards its center, I visualized myself walking backwards in time to my birth, which the center of the figure structure symbolized to me. Then I started slowly following the path from the center back to the outer edge, and that represented when I would die. I retraced my life's journey.

At one point as I was walking along, following the twists and turns of the labyrinth, I was aware that I was trying to coordinate the timing of my exit with when I thought my own life would end. As I moved along the path thinking ahead to the next several turns, I rounded a corner and suddenly found myself leaving the labyrinth. I was startled. I didn't see this coming. I hadn't realized I was that close to the end of my journey.

The labyrinth is not designed to unwind in a simple, straight-forward spiral. Its path is circuitous and unpredictable. The message was clear – we have no way of knowing when we will die. The very next moment could be our last.

Losing Ted so abruptly has helped me to appreciate the precariousness – and the preciousness – of life. Sometimes when I go walking in the natural world these days I say to myself, *If this were to be your last day on earth, you would wish you had taken in the beauty of this exquisite moment.* I look around and notice the light shimmering on the pond, the pair of mallards gliding effortlessly among the reeds, the sparkling of green and gold and orange leaves dancing in the sunlight, the melodious voices of song birds conversing in the tree tops. It helps bring me back to appreciating the richness of life here, this moment, this day. Right here. Right now.

You Don't Ever Have To "Let Go"

"Tell me again, while the last leaves are falling:
'Dear Child, what has been once so interwoven
Cannot be unraveled, nor the gift ungiven.'

Now the dead move through all of us still glowing,
Mother and child, lover and lover mated,
Are wound and bound together and enflowing,
What has been plaited cannot be unplaited--
Only the strands grow richer with each loss
And memory makes kings and queens of us.

Day into light, light into darkness, spin.
When all the birds have flown to some real haven,
We who find shelter in the warmth within,
Listen, and feel new-cherished, new-forgiven
As the lost human voices speak through us and blend
Our complex love, our mourning without end."

May Sarton
"All Souls"

Whenever I hear anyone say, or imply, that I should let go of Ted, I feel my back stiffen. Even though he's been dead for more than ten years, I have a powerful resistance to letting go. I find the whole idea of "letting go" abhorrent. How can I discard someone who has meant life itself to me? It would be like someone saying, "Now that your trip to Machu Picchu and the Amazon Rain Forest is over, you need to forget about it and move on." Why should I do that? Learning to navigate the foreign language, currency and customs and experiencing the spectacular, mystical beauty of the ancient ruins has expanded and deepened me. I was not the same person coming back as the one who went. Being able to call upon these memories makes my life richer. And Peru was only three weeks. I was with Ted for 35 years. He is woven into every fiber of my being. He has become a part of the texture of my life.

As I arrived at the realization that I don't ever have to "let go" of Ted, I felt enormously relieved. Our relationship did not end when he died. In fact, bereavement is just the next phase in our relationship. Just as wedding followed courtship, and then was followed by creating a home, raising and launching our children, emptying the nest and the arrival of grandchildren, so, too, bereavement was waiting its turn. Unknown to us, death was lurking in deep waters, carefully biding its time until at some unexpected moment, as Ted was rowing his boat and pulling hard on the oars, it reared its ugly head and claimed him for its own. Ted and I were happily going along, enjoying the music when suddenly, in mid-measure, the song came to an abrupt halt. But just as surely as night follows day and winter follows autumn, death is not the end of the music, but the next movement in the grand symphony. And like all the other phases, if one handles this transition well, the rewards are great.

Over time, as the waves of sadness have washed away my pain, I've noticed a significant shift. The sharp pangs of missing Ted have greatly diminished, and the grasping for him "out there" somewhere has essentially disappeared. I find that certain events that before would have wrenched me back into the past, now bring a richness of memory. Instead of feeling the ache of his absence, I turn inward and drop into a place within myself – into my heart where he now resides. And there I can saturate myself with his presence – his kind brown eyes that crinkle at the edges, his big wide grin with the one tooth that juts out at an angle, his warm, comforting hand that reaches out for mine.

I can linger in images of him in his workshop happily constructing some kind of gadget; typing away at the computer churning out one of his many ideas; or sitting with a comforting arm around a grandchild and listening intently. When I paddle my kayak on Lake Dillon, or go walking in the woods, or crawl into my bed at night, I can choose to take him with me. I have a wealth of rich, delicious memories I can call upon anytime I want. The sadness has been replaced by a sweet poignancy. When I get in touch with these memories there's no distance at all from the man I loved.

These are not holding-on thoughts. Ted has become a part of me. This could not have happened earlier when I was still in the throes of sadness and longing. With the lifting of sorrow, a barrier has been removed, a barrier to seeing and remembering him clearly. In C. S. Lewis's words:

"You can't see anything properly if your eyes are blurred with tears. . . .
You must have the capacity to receive or the gift can't be given."

Earlier in my grief, my desperate pleas of, *Come to me, Ted, please come to me,* were largely met with silence. The drowning man frantically kicking and clawing cannot be saved. But now that I am pretty well on the other side of grief, I am at a different point. A shift has happened inside of me. Now that my memories are untainted by longing, I can find my husband within myself.

Then there are the times when Ted reaches out to find me. Ted visited me again in a marvelous dream just before this last Thanksgiving. I don't remember the first part of the dream clearly, except that he was with me in a normal, unremarkable way – like I used to feel in the everyday experience of being married to him. Then came the vivid part of the dream:

I had just climbed out of the water – it might have been the shower or a swimming pool (or emerging from my tears and grief). I was dripping wet, just my bare body, and there was Ted standing, fully clothed, smiling and waiting for me. In my playful mood of old, I held a big towel up to Ted's chest and then stepped forward into it, wrapping my soaking body in the towel and his big arms. We hugged and hugged and held each other and kissed and were so happy. I said to him, "Oh Ted, I love you sooo much." And then I added, "I'm so glad we're together again."

I woke up happy, feeling surrounded by his presence.

The next night was the evening before Thanksgiving, and I had driven eight-year-old Skyler and her six-year-old brother, Ian, home to spend the night with me. Ian was sound asleep when we got to my house, and so Skye and I helped him groggily walk up the stairs and snuggled him into bed. It reminded me of the old days when Ted and I arrived home late at night with a car full of sleeping children – carrying them into the house, getting them into their pajamas (or not), tucking them into their beds hoping we could do all this without their becoming fully awake.

After Skye and I had kissed Ian goodnight, we came down to the kitchen and began to play the game of *Quirkle*. Suddenly, the six overhead lights went out and immediately came back on and then about two seconds later went off and stayed off. We both were slightly startled and remarked about it to each other. We could still see to play our game because there were other lights on in the room. But after a couple of minutes I got up and flipped the switch and the six lights came back on. They worked perfectly fine. I didn't want to freak her out, so I didn't say anything about Granddaddy to her, but to me it was just one more confirmation of his ongoing presence. *Thank you, Ted!*

The poet Rainer Maria Rilke's words about his father's death echo mine about Ted's:

> *"Often, in childhood, my thoughts would become confused and my heart would grow numb at the mere idea that sometime he might no longer be; my existence seemed to me so wholly connected to him that to my innermost self his departure seemed like my own doom... But so deep is death implanted in the nature of love that ... it nowhere contradicts love: Where can it drive someone we have borne unutterably in our heart save into this very heart?"*
> Letter to the Countess Margot Sizzo," 1923
> *Letters to a Young Poet*

This brings to mind one day when I decided to brave the wind and freezing cold and go cross-country skiing by myself, I felt the same thrill of adventure and joy in being out in wilderness country that I had felt with Ted countless times in the past. As my skis slid across the frozen terrain, the sensuous experience of skiing with Ted in the high mountains of Colorado echoed back to me.

I remembered our gliding along, following a trail as it wound its way steadily upwards through the pine forest, and then emerged into the sunlight and an enormous snow-covered bowl high above tree line. We had gazed with wonder at the vastness of the snow fields and the craggy peaks that pierced the horizon. Other than a lone bird that soared across the brilliantly blue sky, not a soul was in sight anywhere. There was something compelling about our being out there alone, just the two of us – as if we were experiencing the world before the arrival of humans in all its primordial beauty – awesome, grand, still.

Moments like these that I shared with Ted filled me with awe and put me in touch with something greater. Such experiences have become an undercurrent that flavors and gives meaning to my ongoing life. So now as I ski along, his presence inside me allows me to live more fully in the present. My experiences expand me and help me to better invest in other people and in life. Because I know, as I go through my days, it's not just I, separate little old me, that's living my life, it's US.

Epilogue

Spiral of Grace

"Live in the moment
Love mightily
and bow to the Mystery."

Unknown

Written in 1779 by the English poet John Newton, the song Amazing Grace has been popular through the ages. Before his conversion to Christianity, Newton had worked as a sailor where he gained notoriety for his obscene poems, his profane language and his career in slave trading.

One day, a violent storm battered his ship, and the crew feared they'd capsize. In a moment of desperation, Newton prayed to God for mercy. He knew he could not make it on his own. The ship survived, ultimately leading Newton to give up the slave trading business and become a clergyman. In later life, Newton became an ardent abolitionist and helped end the slave trade in the British Empire.

Newton's hymn, *Amazing Grace,* has always been a favorite of mine. Wikipedia defines Grace as:

"The blessing that comes to us from a divine source regardless of our merit."

Grace is the empowering Presence of God; Grace enables us to be who God created us to be, and to do what He has called us to do. Paul Tillich, wrote in his book, *The Shaking of the Foundations,* that we experience Grace when we are reunited with the Ground of our Being. The opposite of Grace is sin. It is the human condition, our universal fate. Just to be born is to be separated from the Source from which we came, or in Tillich's words, from, *"The mystery, the depth and the greatness of our existence."* Grace is that divine gift that strikes us when we are in great despair and pain, or we are walking through a meaningless and empty life. In his book, *The Shaking of the Foundations*, Tillich writes:

"Sometimes at that moment a wave of light breaks into our darkness, and it is as though a voice were saying 'You are accepted. You are accepted, accepted by that which is greater than you, and the name of which you do not know. Do not ask for the name now; perhaps you will find it later. Do not try to do anything now; perhaps later you will do much...Simply accept the fact that you are accepted! If that

happens to us we experience Grace.' After that, everything is transformed."

As I look back over my life, I realize that Grace has come to me on a handful of momentous occasions. Each time, Grace appeared unbidden in the form of a loving relationship with someone who cared. Every instance turned out to be life altering in a fundamental way. On each occasion, a door was opened and I was offered an opportunity to enter a whole new dimension of being. It was like I had reached a crossroads and was forced to face a major decision: do I turn away in fear and continue down the old, familiar, "safe" path, or will I gather my courage, take the big step and walk through that door? I have had to make a choice; I have had to do my part.

Most of these occasions of Grace meeting me occurred during moments of extreme tension where I sensed, on some intuitive level, that my decision would be life changing. Hidden possibilities awaited me if I chose the unknown path. I have written about all of these moments of Grace – except for one – earlier in the book.

Amazing Grace! How sweet the sound that saved a wretch like me.

My dear grandmother was the first significant person to bring Grace to me and to make a profound difference in the trajectory of my life. She was there with me from the beginning. I was a scared, insecure little girl until we drove through the gates of my grandparents' Colorado ranch and I was with Pags and Grama again. My part was easy. All I had to do was crawl up into Grama's welcoming arms and settle into the soft folds of her lap. Her warmth and caresses gave me the gift of a childhood that allowed me to be innocent and trusting, joyful and carefree.

I once was lost but now am found, was blind but now I see.

The next person whose loving presence made a life altering difference to me was my Graduate School of Social Work supervisor. When LaVerne asked me to write an autobiography of my life, I sensed she was opening a door, one where I could find a whole new way of being. Until then, I had tried to hide the shame of my father's alcoholism behind a surface veneer of perfectionism while trying to "be nice."

I told Laverne my real story. Instead of trying to impress LaVerne with my accomplishments, I took a big risk, not knowing how she'd react. It was such a wonder to me that she did accept me – all of me. Not just my accomplished side, but my dark side, too; *especially* my dark side. The reason it was my dark side was because I'd kept it hidden, in the dark. It was my human side.

Each encounter with Grace made it possible for me to take the next transformative step. If I hadn't become more comfortable with my human side, I wouldn't have been ready for a Ted Anderson to walk into my life. In trusting LaVerne I also had become more able to trust my intuition and learned to take some risks. When that tall, lanky, young man with the boyish smile appeared suddenly in the hallway where I worked and asked me out to the movies – and then two dates later invited me to go on a weekend camping trip with him and his children – a part of me wanted to run in the other direction. In the sixties, spending an overnight with a man – let alone someone you've just had two dates with – just wasn't done. It also felt risky because I was still a rather anxious, insecure young woman, and I feared that this man, whom I so admired, wouldn't like me if he got to know me. But once again I chose to walk through that open door. I had fallen in love with Ted on that first date; I sensed somehow this man was different. The rest is history as they say – or at least was my history for the next 35 years. His sudden death caused him to depart from my life as precipitously as he'd entered it. Ted brought romantic love and the gift of four amazing children to my life.

I want to add here that each child in his or her own right was also an act of Grace. Choosing to marry a man with two seven-year-old twins was taking a big step. I made a decision to walk through the door of instant motherhood. Then two years later we decided to have another child, and then six months later another. Within four years I'd become a wife and mother to four children of varying ages and stages. Parenthood for Ted and me was challenging at times, but so worth it. Each of my children and my eight grandchildren is unique and brings such joy to my life. I am forever grateful I took that leap of faith so many years ago and went on that camping trip.

**'*Twas Grace that taught my heart to fear and Grace my fears relieved.*
*How precious did that Grace appear the hour I first believed.***

When I first read the beginning line of this second stanza, I didn't understand it. It was Grace that taught my heart to *fear*? Why would Grace do such an awful thing? Why would Grace take away my precious husband? But as I learned to go on after Ted's death and struggled to make meaning of this tragedy, I was determined not only to survive losing him, but to somehow gain something from it. The horrible times I went through propelled me into worlds of discovery that were only made possible by his dying. And so, yes, it was also Grace that plunged me into the darkest times in my life. The rest was up to me.

Someone recently asked me, "So, what was the turning point? What helped you to heal and be open to life again?" There was no one moment in time when I turned the corner. It was a gradual process.

Several threads came together to re-weave the torn fabric of my life. The first was that I allowed myself to really grieve. Time and time again, the tears would bubble up from deep in my chest and pour out of my eyes. *I did not hold them back.* Gradually, the periods between the waves of sadness lengthened and the intensity of sorrow lessened.

Ultimately most of the pain has washed away and I am now left with vivid, poignant memories of the man I loved. I rarely yearn for my dead husband who is missing "out there" somewhere. Instead, I can find him, whenever I want, residing deeply within my heart. His presence within me is like an undercurrent that enriches and gives meaning to my ongoing life.

Another gift I've received from weathering the storms of grief is that my heart can now easily expand to experience other intense emotions. As it had to enlarge to contain the enormity of my sadness, it has been stretched over time. Now that the sadness is largely gone, I am able to be as deeply moved by something beautiful, tender and joyful as by something sad.

One very important factor in my healing was the comfort and courage I gained from other people – whether it was the unfailing love and support of my family and friends or the sharing with my psychotherapist and my widow buddies. I learned that the secret to feeling better when I am sad or lonely is to pick up the phone and reach out to someone else who might also be going through a tough time. It always works.

Since childhood, I have loved to read. When Ted died, it was natural for me to turn to books. I devoured the stories written by other widows, and there I learned many useful survival tips and gained messages of hope from others who had suffered terrible losses, but had gone on to thrive and be happy.

As I read, the nature of my interests expanded and my focus of reading expanded as well. Since I had experienced a number of extraordinary events after Ted died – the rainbows, the bears on Mt. Washington, the strange behavior of electrical lights, the many incredible dreams, and the fascinating visits with mediums – I was drawn towards books on After Death Communication, Near Death Experiences and other books exploring the frontiers of science.

My meeting the Buddhist therapist on Southwest Airlines shortly after Ted's death was another appearance of Grace in my life. Resulting from this encounter, I became interested in spirituality – mysticism and Eastern religion, in particular. With the hope of learning more about death and what happens to us after we die, I read numerous books, attended workshops and joined a Buddhist meditation group. As I studied the various religions, I found that, though they are different in a myriad of ways, a single universal truth shines at the core of every religion, and that is *Love*. *Love* is the most important thing. This certainly resonated with my experience. In my recovery from grief, I found that caring *about and for each other* is what makes all the difference. Closely related to the idea of Love is the concept of Oneness.

"Love thy neighbor as thyself " because thy neighbor *is* myself.

If we look at each other, we can be aware of all our surface differences. We can view the world through the lens of our ego, and feel separate and alienated as we compete, compare and judge. This is what Tillich speaks of in his sermon, when he says that we are all estranged from our Source, from the *Ground of our Being*. Certainly when Ted died I felt lonely, set apart from others and absorbed in my own sorrow. But mysticism, the Eastern religions and progressive Christianity teach that at the deepest level we all come from the same Source. A spark of The Divine dwells within every living being. We are all One. We are all connected.

Earlier in this book, I told the story of the gift I received from the blind woman whom I had observed in Starbucks one day. She was another moment of Grace in my life because it was through her that I realized we are all One. At the deepest level everyone wants to be happy; everyone wants to be treated with dignity and everyone wants to be loved.

I found all these ideas helpful, and they'd all begun coming to me on the journey I'd started so many years earlier when LaVerne entered my life. I feel a sense of Oneness with life and feel connected to everyone. I have compassion for us all, wherever we are on this journey through life.

As I look back now, I believe that I was spiraling my way out of the depths of despair and grief after Ted's death. Each experience of Grace helped better prepare me to receive the next; each one brought me further along towards reuniting with *"the mystery, the depth and greatness of our existence,"* which Tillich wrote about.

And thus, I healed.

I found happiness with life again; I developed a circle of good friends; I enjoyed many fulfilling activities; and I no longer needed to search for a man. I was grateful that I'd had a "love of my life," and, in fact, I occasionally commented that my wish for everyone is that they might have – once in their lifetime – a *"love of their life."* I believed I'd had my quota.

Grace Appears Again

But nearly a dozen years after Ted's death, Grace appeared – again. Just as magically as Ted had walked into my life, a new man appeared. Actually, Ted and I had known Ken and his wife, Louise, for more than fifteen years through a tennis group we belonged to. Ken and his wife came to Ted's memorial service, and then, when Louise died, I went to her service. As Ken was facing those dark times of his own early grief, he reached out to me in order to learn how I had dealt with the loss of a beloved spouse.

One day as we were having dinner, he paused, straightened his plate on his placemat, looked at me with his tender, blue eyes and spoke.

"You know, Cindy, I'm beginning to like you."

I was stunned! I had not seen this coming! I was swept away by a rush of my own emotions. From that moment, I was smitten. Since I'd already had one "love of my life," I didn't know it was possible to actually fall in love again. But I'm here to tell you that, yes, you can. And that is why I put the bumper sticker on the back of my car, **Grace Happens.**

Actually, this momentous event had begun much earlier in the day. On that particular day, I was going to be playing tennis before going to Ken's house for dinner. I remember walking into my bedroom to get changed, and flipping on the wall switch in order to turn on the light. But the lamp didn't go on. My first thought was that my cleaning lady must have turned off the light by turning off the switch on the lamp, rather than by the switch on the wall. However, when I tried to turn the light on by its own switch, it still wouldn't go on. So I figured that bulb must've burned out.

I got a new bulb and screwed it in, but the light still didn't go on. I then realized that the other two lamps in the room that were connected to the same wall switch hadn't gone on either. So I guessed that the extension cord must have become unplugged. I started to pull the dresser away from the wall to see if the cord was still plugged in. But realizing my time constraint, I thought, *I don't have time for this now. I'll deal with this when I come home.*

I went and played tennis. When I came home and walked into my bedroom, I discovered all three lights were shining brightly! I was surprised. Now if this had been the first time that the electricity had behaved strangely, I would have written it off as just an anomaly. Since it had occurred once again, at a critically significant time – when I was about to go off and meet the man I was destined to fall in love with – I was inclined to think it was a part of the mystery. Perhaps Ted's energy or spirit was sending me the message, "This is it, honey! Go for it! You have my blessing."

Since that day, which at this writing was well over a year ago, there have been no more unusual electrical events. I sometimes think that Ted, after completing this final task of taking care of me, may have gone back to his job of doing whatever dead people do.

Over the months, as Ken and I have continued to date each other, our love has deepened, and we have gone on to build an exciting new life together. We each sold our homes and purchased a new home overlooking a gorgeous lake. It has been magical.

We often have remarked to each other that if we hadn't had such loving relationships with our spouses, we wouldn't have been able to go on to feel love and tenderness for each other.

I had a most remarkable realization many months after Ken and I became a couple: he actually does pass the shoe test. Until I re-read the Cinderella Story chapter of the book, I'd forgotten the dream I'd had years ago about trying shoes on potential romantic partners and not being able to find anyone who could wear Ted's size 13 shoes. Like Ted, Ken wears a size 13 shoe!

Before I end, I want to tell you about an amazing dream I had shortly after Ken and I decided to buy our new home overlooking the pond:

I was swimming. Swimming, alone and upstream. The going was tough. I pulled and pulled, stroke after stroke, struggling against the current. I couldn't tell if I was making any headway, but I just kept on going. There was no other choice. Sometimes the river flattened out, sometimes the water became turbulent and the current became stronger. The air was getting colder and before I knew it, the water had turned icy.

I found myself now swimming on top of the ice, still doing the breast-stroke. I kept pulling, and I kept slowly sliding myself across the ice. I was becoming exhausted; I had about reached my limit. And then, in the distance, I began to see the sky brightening and the water opening up into an enormous lake. By now the ice had disappeared and I began to catch a glimmer of a most amazing sight.

At about that time in the dream, I glanced off to my right and saw that I was passing my grandparent's ranch. Grama was waving to me from the shore. I was

177

drawn back to the lake and continued to swim ahead. A shimmering silvery mist hung over the water; it was the most magical, the most gorgeous scene I had ever viewed. A vast lake stretched out as far as I could see. It was expansive, utterly tranquil and stunningly beautiful. I was filled with joy.

When I awoke, the message in the dream was clear. After a tough upstream battle through the challenges of grief, I had ultimately arrived at a place of great peace and joy – my new life with Ken in our home overlooking the pond. This mirrored the experience I'd had so many years ago, of arriving at the ranch – and my grandparent's welcoming arms – after a difficult struggle to move through the darkness, turbulence and fear of my parent's home. Similarly, John Newton, centuries earlier, re-counted in his poem, *Amazing Grace* how, after weathering the violent storms that threatened to destroy him, he was blessed with the most amazing Grace that, in time, became life changing.

Who knows what makes it possible for you to fall in love with someone, <u>and</u> for that person to fall in love with you? Countless books have been written about this most elusive of subjects, this most sought after of all events, and yet, it still remains a Mystery.

I call it Grace.

When we've been here ten thousand years, bright shining as the sun,
We've no less days to sing God's praise than when we'd first begun.

Bibliography

Almaas, A.H. *The Inner Journey Home, Soul's Realization of the Unity of Reality.* Boston, MA: Shambhala, 2004.

Anderson, George. *Lessons from the Light, Extraordinary Messages of Comfort and Hope from the Other Side,* Berkeley, CA: Penguin Putnam, Inc., 1999.

Armstrong, Karen. *The Great Transformation, the Beginning of our Religious Traditions.* New York: Knopf Books, 2006.

Banks, Coleman. *A Year with Rumi: Daily Readings.* New York: Broadway Books, 2006.

Banks, Coleman. *The Essential Rumi, New Expanded Edition* (translated by Moyne, John). New York: Barnes and Noble, 2004.

Banks, Coleman. *The Illuminated Rumi.* New York: Broadway Books, 1997.

Blackman, Sushila (ed.) *Graceful Exits, How Great Beings Die, Death Stories of Tibetan, Hindu and Zen Masters.* Trumbull, CT: Weatherhill, 1997.

Blum, Deborah. *Ghost Hunters, William James and the Search for Scientific Proof of Life After Death.* New York: Penguin Press, 2006.

Boom, Corrie Ten. *Clippings from My Notebook.* Nashville, Tennessee:Thomas Nelson, Inc., 1982.

Botkin, Allan L. *Induced After Death Communication, a New Therapy for Healing Grief and Trauma.* Charlottesville, VA: Hampton Roads Publ., CA., 2005.

Campbell, Joseph. (ed.) *"On Synchronicity," The Portable Jung,* New York: Viking Penguin, 1971.

Chopra, Deepak. *The Book of Secrets, Unlocking the Hidden Dimensions of Your Life.* New York: Harmony Books, 2004.

Chopra, Deepak. *Buddha, a Story of Enlightenment.* San Francisco: HarperCollins Public, 1997.

Chopra, Deepak. *Life After Life, the Burden of Proof.* New York: Three Rivers Press, 2006.

Chodron, Pema. *When Things Fall Apart.* Boston: Shambala Public, Inc., 1997.

Dalai Lama. *Dzogchen, Heart Essence of the Great Perfection.* New York: Snow Lion Publications, 2000.

Davis, John V. The Diamond Approach. *An Introduction to the Teachings of A. H. Almaas,* Boston: Shambhala Public. Inc., 1999.

Didion, Joan. *The Year of Magical Thinking.* New York: Knopf, 2005.

Dogen. *Zen and the Art of Anything.* Columbia, South Carolina: Summerhouse Press, 1999.

Erdich, Louise. *The Painted Drum.* New York: Harper Perennial, 2006.

Ericcson, Stephanie. *Companion Through the Darkness.* New York: Harper Collins, 1993.

Gibran, Kahlil. *The Prophet.* Oxford, England: Oneworld Public, 1998.

Ginsburg, Genevieve Davis. *Widow to Widow.* Cambridge, MA: Da Capo Press, 1995.

Goldstein, Joseph and Jack Kornfield. *Seeking the Heart of Wisdom, the Path of Insight Meditation.* Boston: Shambhala, 1987.

Goodwin, Doris Kearns. *Team of Rivals,* Simon and Schuster, 2005.

Grosse, Ray. "Synchronicity and the Mind of God", *Quest,* May-June, 2006. p. 92.

Guggenheim, Judy and Bill. *Hello from Heaven,* New York: Bantam Books, 1995.

Hall, Donald. *Without.* Boston: Houghton Mifflin Co., 1998.

Heathcote-James. *After-Death Communication.* London: Metro Publishing, 2008.

Holland, John. *Born Knowing, A Medium's Journey, Accepting and Embracing my Spiritual Gifts.* New York: Hay House, Inc., 2003.

Holland, John. *The Spirit Whisperer, Chronicles of a Medium.* New York: Hay House, Inc., 2010.

Holmes, Ernest. *The Science of Mind.* New York: Penguin Putnam Inc., 1998.

Humphreys, Christmas. *Exploring Buddhism.* Wheaton, IL: The Theosophical Publishing House, 1974.

Kabat-Zinn, Jon. *Coming to our Senses, Healing Ourselves and the World Through Mindfulness.* New York: Hyperion, 2005.

Kempton, Sally. *Meditation for the Love of It.* Boulder, CO: Sounds True Inc., 2011.

Kornfield, Jack. *A Path with Heart, a Guide through the Perils and Promises of Spiritual Life.* New York: Bantam Books, 1993.

Kubler-Ross, Elisabeth. *On Death and Dying.* New York: Macmillan Publ. Co., 1969.

Kubler-Ross, Elisabeth. *The Tunnel and the Light, Essential Insights on Living and Dying.* New York: Marlowe and Co., 1999.

Kubler-Ross, Elisabeth. *The Wheel of Life, a Memoir of Living and Dying.* New York: Scribner, 1997.

Kunitz, Stanley. *The Collected Poems.* "The Long Boat." New York: Norton and Co., 2000.

LeShan, Lawrence. *The Medium, the Mystic and the Physicist, Toward a General Theory of the Paranormal."* New York: Viking Press, 1974.

Levine, Stephen. *Who Dies? An Investigation of Conscious Living and Conscious Dying.* New York: Anchor Books, 1982.

Mayer Ph.D., Elizabeth Lloyd. *Extraordinary Knowing, Science, Skepticism, and the Inexplicable Powers of the Human Mind.* New York: Bantam Books, 2007.

Mitchell, Stephen. *Bhagavad Gita.* New York: Random House, 2000.

Moody, Raymond A. *Life after Life.* Covington, Georgia: Mockingbird Books, 1973.

Moss, Robert. *Conscious Dreaming.* New York: Three Rivers Press, 1996.

Murdoch, Iris. *The Sacred and Profane Love Machine*. New York, NY: Grand Central Publishing, 1975.

Neimeyer, Robert. *Meaning Reconstruction and the Experience of Loss*. Wash. D.C.: the American Psychological Assoc., 2001.

Neruda, Pablo. *100 Love Sonnets*. "Sonnet XCIV." Toronto, Canada: Exile Editions, Ltd., 1986.

Nietzsche, Friedrich. *Twilight of the Idols and Anti-Christ.* London: Penguin Books, 1990.

Nye, Naomi Shihab. *Words Under the Words: Selected Poems*. "Kindness." Portland, Oregon: Eighth Mountain Press, 1995.

Occhiogrosso, Peter. *Joy of Sects*. New York: Doubleday Dell Publ., 1996.

Oliver, Mary. *New and Selected Poems*. "When Death Comes." Boston: Beacon Press, 1992.

Prendergast, John (ed.) *The Sacred Mirror, Nondual Wisdom and Psychotherapy*. St. Paul, MN: Paragon House, 2003.

Ram Das. *Be Here Now*, CA: Three Rivers Press, 1971.

Raymo, Chet. *Natural Prayers.* St. Paul, MN: Hungry Mind Press, 1999.

Remen, Rachel Naomi. "Glimpse of a Deeper Order. " Shambala Sun, Nov. 2000.

Remen, Rachel Naomi. *Kitchen Table Wisdom, Stories that Heal.* New York: Riverhead Books, 1996.

Rilke, Rainer Maria (translated by Harmon, Mark). *Letters to a Young Poet*, Cambridge: Harvard University Press, 2011.

Rinpoche, Sogyal. *The Tibetan Book of Living and Dying*. San Fransisco, CA: HarperCollins Publ., 1994.

Romanyshyn, Robert. *The Soul in Grief, Love, Death and Transformation*. Berkeley, CA: North Atlantic Books, 1999.

Rosenberg, Larry. *Breath by Breath, The Liberating Practice of Insight Meditation.* New York: Shambhala, 1998.

Salzberg, Sharon. *Faith.* New York: Riverhead Books, 2002.

Sarton, May. *In Time Like Air.* "All Souls." New York: Rinehart and Co, 1958.

Schupp, Linda J. *Grief: Normal, Complicated, Traumatic.* WI: PESI, 2003.

Schwartz, Gary E. *The Afterlife Experiments, Breakthrough Scientific Evidence of Life After Death.* New York: Atria Books, 2002.

Shakespeare, William. *Shakespeare's Comedies, Histories, and Tragedies,* "The Tragedy of Macbeth." London: Blount and Jaggard, 1623.

St. Vincent Millay, Edna. As quoted by Nancy Milford in *Savage Beauty: the Life of Edna St. Vincent Millay, New York: Random House, 2002.*

Sumedho, Ajahn. *The Sound of Silence.* Somerville, MA: Wisdom Public, 2007.

Swanson, John L. *Communing with Nature, a Guidebook for Enhancing Your Relationship with the Living Earth.* Oregon: Illahee Press, 2001.

Tagore, Rabindranath. *Fireflies.* New York, NY: Macmillan Co. Publishers, 1975.

Tarrant, John. *The Light Inside the Dark.* New York: Harper Collins Publ., 1998.

Thich Nhat Hanh. *Call Me by My True Names.* Berkeley, CA: Parallax Press, 1999.

Thurman, Robert. *The Jewel Tree of Tibet, The Enlightenment Engine of Tibetan Buddhism.* New York: Simon & Schuster, 2005.

Tolle, Eckhart. *A New Earth.* New York: Penguin Group, 2005.

Vaughan-Lee, Llewellyn. *Working with Oneness.* Inverness, CA: The Golden Sufi Center, 2002.

Wagoner, David. *Collected Poems 1956-1976.* "Lost." Bloomington, Indiana: Indiana University Press, 1976.

Walsh, Neale Donald. *Conversations with God*, Charlottesville, VA: Hampton Roads Public. Co., 1998.

Williams Margery. *The Velveteen Rabbit*, New York: Random House, 1958.

Wray, T. J. *Grief Dreams, How They Help Heal Us After the Death of a Loved One*. San Fransisco, CA: Jossey Bass, 2005.

Acknowledgements

This book would not have come into being without the support and wisdom of many people. I am indebted to my two editors: Ruth Herman, Founder and Director of the Circle of Writers in Acton, MA, and Peter Occhiogrosso, who specializes in Eastern Spirituality. I also thank my memoir writing coach, Tom Daley, for his writing expertise and enthusiasm for my project. Much gratitude and thanks go to Barbara Pizer, who helped me keep my feet on the ground and hope in my heart. I am also deeply grateful for my *Good Grief* Group and to my dear friends, all who traveled this road with me. Together we cried, we laughed and helped each other to know we are not alone. I am especially appreciative of my family for their unwavering love and support and to Ken Kreutziger for his encouragement, his love and his presence in my life.

Cynthia Peabody Anderson, LICSW, was born on June 18, 1941, in Denver, Colorado. After attending college and graduate schools in Colorado, she began her professional career as a clinical social worker in Palo Alto, California. It was there that she met Theodore I. Anderson, MD, a young psychiatrist who had recently been widowed. Two years later, they were married and Cindy became the instant mother of Ted's seven year-old twins, Scott and Sandy. After a short honeymoon in Hawaii, the family moved to Massachusetts where Ted had accepted a position as Assistant Commissioner of Mental Health. Two years later a little girl, Karyn, was born and a year later a son, Brett, arrived. Cindy has continued to work as a psychotherapist in private practice where she specializes in treating adults with anxiety, depression, grief, trauma and marital issues. It was the day after Ted and Cindy celebrated their 33rd wedding anniversary that Ted died suddenly after crossing the finish line while rowing in a 2,000 m. singles sculling event. Cindy resides in Lexington, MA, with her new partner, Ken Kreutziger. In this book she writes about the challenges and triumphs of those intervening twelve years.

Made in the USA
Charleston, SC
10 September 2015